DISPENSING WEALTH AND WISDOM
FOR DREAMERS, THINKERS, MAVERICKS,
SEEKERS, AND STRIVERS!

# SIMPLE RICH PEOPLE

SHEKHAR CHOPRA

EDITED BY DIYA CHOPRA

SIMPLE RICH PEOPLE
Copyright © 2024 by Shekhar Chopra. All rights reserved.

**MINDSTIR MEDIA**

Published by MindStir Media, LLC
45 Lafayette Rd | Suite 181| North Hampton, NH 03862 | USA
1.800.767.0531 | www.mindstirmedia.com
Printed in the United States of America.
ISBN Paperback: 978-1-961532-23-6

To my Grandfather

Wishwanath Chopra

A maverick, a visionary, a guide, a troublemaker, a pioneer, a walker,
an independent and courageous spirit in deeds and in words,
and a doting grandfather.

# CONTENTS

# INTRODUCTION
# FROM THE AUTHOR

Simple Rich People shows people how to build wealth. Wealth earned the right way is a significant impetus for self-belief. Wealth is not only described by the amount of money one has, though this is a metric that helps measure, but it's also a shameless quantitative metric. Wealth is not what it is but what it can provide to the individual in pursuit of this highly prized yet mostly elusive reward.

This book shares simple principles to generate wealth. Seemingly ordinary people can achieve incredible wealth through simplicity and ingenuity. Someone's genes determine neither simplicity nor ingenuity; these are within the sphere of influence of "ordinary" human beings. Ordinary human is an oxymoron akin to corporate well-being and work-life balance. Corporate well-being feels like a resort spa experience. And work-life balance is a myth to follow to hell — burn your work and your life. The banal truth is that there is only life, and work in any form supports this life. There is no ordinary human being. Each human being is a trapeze artist, a magician in an invisible cloak. Endowed with unique abilities, we have sufficient assets within ourselves to create wealth with purpose.

The principles in the book will take you from A to Z for creating wealth, the state of A being where you are today even if you are starting out under mountains of debt. And Z is where you want to go. For those who lean quantitatively, the number is yours to pick. I cannot guarantee whether you will reach this number, but if you choose it wisely you have my assurance of a life well lived and money well beyond your needs.

The book provides details of the process of becoming wealthy, metrics to monitor, spending areas to focus on, tips on learning and growth, and career development that will complement your journey and open avenues for advancement.

First, a bit about myself, I am an immigrant, an American, who arrived as collateral damage with my father, an astute, ethical banker. He came to the United States to expand business operations for his employer. My father was a top academic performer and a non-political statesman who stoically performed his duty at home and at work. At home, he was the kindest man with a caring demeanor. Both of his kids, especially I, the eldest, took advantage of his calm and understanding nature. Not the most expressive with his words, his deeds professed his love for his family. An atheist in the largest democracy, his ethical conduct was beyond reproach. I was taken to task by him a total of three times, all for the same reason. I showed disrespect to my mother. Disrespecting any other woman would have qualified for the same punishment. Every time he hit me, it was a smack, and I felt like a Greek general getting pounded by Obelix. My father was tall like Obelix but of a thin frame.

Other people laid the foundation of who I am, my vocation, and my penchant for a life of liberty gained through wealth. My paternal grandfather, a brilliant man, had to flee for his life from fear of religious persecution. Still, in his mid-nineties, he has never stopped contributing to the community. His eccentric manner confounded family, friends, and society alike. In life, as in common folklore, the renegades, the oppressed, the underdogs, and the belittled often beat the odds and make a life for themselves. He was a good-looking man of sturdy proportions. Being his eldest grandchild and strongly resembling him, he often doted on me and realized I was more like him than just the pigmentation.

So, he took me under his wing and taught me all he knew about life. His views were authentic and insightful and at odds with the behaviors of the masses. He was an honest man. For this quaint peculiarity, he had limited friends, but many sought his oft-bitter advice. He was a visionary, an unassuming man true to himself and oblivious, by design and primarily by purpose, to the judgment of those around him. He taught me about culture, people, money, and the philosophies of life that only a doting grandfather can provide. Much of it while walking. Those walks with him shaped my views about life, money, and culture. His most valuable lesson to me was a willingness to be fiercely independent and follow ambitious, long-shot, self-determined goals with vigor and passion.

My mother, a woman of short frame and tall stature, taught me the strength of a life lived with perseverance and grit. She taught me about women's struggles and instilled an expectation to support a world that promotes equal opportunity for all. She was open about her struggles as a woman in the domestic fabric of raising kids in India and her professional career. An entire chapter in this book is about creating wealth in a woman's world.

Many others influenced me, too many to list, and each would merit a few pages. An independent maternal aunt, a teacher in Los Angeles who paved the way for my college, and a gangster who saved my life are among them. I have also had the privilege of learning from a renowned teacher. As I write this, this teacher is unaware of this particular student. Mr. Warren Buffett's teachings and annual letters have made a positive and impressionable impact. Like my grandfather, Mr. Buffett's wise tales and manner of conduct have influenced the principles in this book.

Many characters in this book reflect habits of people I know. I have sprinkled a dash of creative liberty with the stories to make it entertaining and relatable.

A sensible and sagacious man once said, "Rules are for the guidance of the wise and obedience of fools." Please use the rules in this book to build your life's strong foundation, not with eyes wide shut but ears wide open. Don't be afraid to experiment, improvise, pivot. Just don't lose faith. The principles work. It's a journey. It will not be easy, but if you come along on this adventure, you will grow in stature and substance.

# CHAPTER 1

# FROM A TO Z

Bonjour, you are at Stop A today. In the present, in the moment. Whether you have a significant debt that keeps you awake at night or believe you know everything about finance and sleep well at night, you are at this bus stop. People of all backgrounds are at this bus stop with you. You may be a college student thinking about the cute guy you will meet in journalism class or a single mother worried about funding her kid's college education. You may be a program analyst who just got the news that she got laid off, or you may be a mega millions lottery winner. You are at Stop A.

Business executives, janitors, priests, doctors, teachers, politicians, the homeless, students, and teenagers, you are at Stop A. Mothers, fathers, aunts, uncles, brothers, sisters, friends, stepmothers, stepfathers, frenemies, BFFs, sons, daughters, in-laws, you are at Stop A. Americans, Tanzanians, Armenians, Indians, Swiss, Japanese, Nigerians, Saudi Arabians, Canadians, Russians, Koreans, Brazilians, French, and Greeks, you are at Stop A. Single, separated, divorced, married, engaged, you are at Stop A. Clear-purposed, still figuring out, always confused, you are at Stop A.

Stop A is getting rather crowded. And well, the bus stop is figurative. In concrete terms, you are at a train station. And we are all waiting for this train. And as one enters this train, the conductor, a stern woman of 5 feet 1 inch and healthy proportions, looks with her piercing eyes and asks a simple direct question. "Are you here to travel to Z?" The passengers know she means business. You can feel the electricity within her; as she communicates, she zaps energy from the universe and connects. Remarkably, not one person says no. However, it is imperative that each yes comes out of their volition. So, she asks everyone on the train the same set of questions. "Are you here to travel to Z? Are you sure?" And finally a welcome statement, "Good. Sit tight and enjoy the ride. Our next and final stop is Z."

And then the train departs. Soon, the commotion of the train station is an afterthought. A concoction of apprehension and uncertainty clouds many passengers' minds. As the train departs, the passengers see the murky skies above with the ravenous, barren mountains outside the train station. And then once in a while a gleam of hope comes. And the landscape changes, revealing the lush green grass outside with a blue sky and a blue ocean or a starry night with space enough for all the worries of the universe to coalesce in a single blot of energy.

And soon, the passengers start talking with one another, and small talk often veers toward the weather. And then the realization seeps through and spreads like wildfire. A realization that the weather outside is a projection of their imagination. The rugged jaunty cliffs, the vast barren land, and the sunlight that peers through murky forests of green are all a projection. Our thoughts create a subjective world that mirrors our reality. And as the passengers realize this, something remarkable starts happening. There is a lot more sunlight. The opacity of the dark forests starts trickling with sun rays and birds chirping, and an occasional beautiful park or gushing waterfall comes into view. In the distance, kids are laughing and playing. Museums are sprouting. A shopping mall only rises for an architect. Isn't it quaint that where we often spend time to relieve our boredom is never the place that arises for our aspirations and dreams?

Some of the passengers then feel comfortable moving in the train. Though at first sight, it would have been hard to imagine a vehicle carrying this crowded ensemble having enough space, but once you are inside the train and willing to stretch out of your volition the train seems to have a mind and body of its own. The train expands to accommodate the passengers' desires to stretch and move around. All the passengers have to do is try. The space listens. Some of the passengers start realizing this oddity. The first ones to learn of this capability are usually those who have a deeper connection to themselves. Then some early adopters nudge others to follow in their footsteps and discover the truisms of this magical train.

So, slowly and nonchalantly, the people start moving, stretching, and jumping, like a newborn, as if they are engaging the world for the first time. A new avatar of novel experience is born from their willingness to engage, experiment, and explore, devoid of any external triggers or substance use. As there is movement, the landscape outside changes to reflect more lush greens, the orange sun rises, the blue-sky yawns and expands, and a vibrancy erupts. The chirp of birds gains momentum as if they have joined in this march toward consciousness.

As people feel more comfortable and confident, they leave for other compartments and mingle with passengers. And then some passengers reach the last compartment. This chamber has music emanating from the inside, a piece of soothing, inviting music that touches the heart and energizes the soul. Upon entering this compartment, a gush of wind picks up the entrants and floats them as if on a hoverboard. They can see that this chamber has no enclosures, it's open on both sides, and they can hover inside and outside. Outside! And clouds are floating. This train compartment isn't on a horizontal track; it's lunging forward and upward, merging with the clouds. People can move in and out of the train at any time, just hovering and being one with the consciousness around them, aware of their individuality and yet connected with the collective. And up there is a constellation of stars that can be seen in the daylight resembling a "Z."

# CHAPTER 2

# THE WHY: FINANCIAL EMPOWERMENT

Reaching Z is not an end. It is a state of being. The State of Z is not a destination but a journey. It is a journey toward liberation, toward harnessing your true self. The station of Z delivers a feeling of financial empowerment. The individual feels empowered not to worry about money while making life choices. Financially empowered individuals do not smoke weed all day and quit their day jobs. Quite to the contrary, they engage in meaningful activities, often make much money, and drive impact. They fit their career or business into their lives, not vice versa. Many financially empowered individuals live their lives true to themselves and their purpose. They are more engaged with their families and kids and create an environment around them where their kids, spouses, relatives, friends, and coworkers gain benefits from their presence and their behaviors. They tend to live in domiciles they feel good about, stay married because of love and grow old with their spouse, take care of the gift of good health, and are patriotic because they feel gratitude and want to leave a stronger nation to the future generations. These Z-induced people give money to the groups they belong to, religious and otherwise. They pursue hobbies and academics because they want to keep learning and growing. Though such people are not oblivious to financial transactions, they do not view money as a hindrance but as what money represents: a medium to simplify the give and take.

For the statistically inclined, a few tidbits follow.

- A third of adults with partners report that money is a significant source of conflict in their relationship.[1] Nearly three-quarters (72 percent) report feeling stressed about money at least some of the time, and about one-quarter (22 percent) say they experienced extreme stress about money during the past month.1

- More than half of adults (54 percent) say they have just enough or not enough money to make ends meet at the end of the month.

- Nearly 1 in 5 Americans say that they have either considered skipping or skipped going to the doctor in the past year when they needed health care because of health concerns.

Financial stress becomes more acute for lower income levels, parents, and younger generations. Women consistently report higher stress levels than men and appear more challenging to cope with. These patterns flow into their relationship with money and finances. Nearly half of women (49 percent) say that paying for essentials is a somewhat or very significant source of stress, compared with 38% of men.

With women gaining a stronger foothold financially at home and work, women have a mammoth opportunity to leverage the hard-earned progress achieved over the last hundred years to benefit their lives and experience less anxiety. As some of you have undoubtedly noticed, there is a paradox here. Why are women, who have gained so much over the last hundred years, much more anxious? Naked ambition? When you progress, you get attached to it, and anxiety arises over whether that progress is sustainable. That is, the potential loss of progress or even the perceived slowness of the rate of progress in the future causes stress.

The persistent anxiousness of many wealthy and ultra-rich people also stems from the same fear. Though these people may be objectively rich, they are not at Station Z. Financial empowerment is not the same as being wealthy. Wealth helps gain financial empowerment, but one must know when enough is enough. A feeling of flight and levity accompanies the energizing ambiance of feeling satisfied and motivated. It is a flight to one's path of one's choosing. Even the fastest car will not match the speed of a plane. Being financially empowered is a state of awareness where money becomes a non-issue for living your life. It's not a number, though knowledge and understanding of your wealth is a prerequisite. Simple metrics covered in the next chapter will guide you to this state. If you are a wealthy person worried about money, you are not benefiting from the good feeling that financial empowerment bestows upon you, though I congratulate you on your wealth, especially if you made it yourself ethically. You are well ahead of the curve.

Being empowered is not the same as being a millionaire. For some, it could be more; for others, it could be less. Empowerment comes in a package with fiscal responsibility. That is paying your bills on time, paying your taxes, and treating your friends and family fairly. And why wouldn't you? If truly financially empowered, why would you hold money as a power play over or mistreat others? True liberation is about willingness to give and share and knowing that character development is the fruit of the labor. Helping someone or guiding others is not a way to make us feel more powerful but an opportunity to make us better people and build a connected world on this blue planet.

There is no better way to harness the power of humanity than to empower women and liberate half the world to march in search of reaching their potential. A society that empowers our mothers, sisters, wives, daughters, daughters-in-law, friends, and coworkers is a society that will propel men forward as well. It raises the bar for men. Talented, intelligent women are not looking to date sloppy Joe, who lives in the basement of his parents' house. Of course, you may be a billionaire, and your date may still find ways to improve you. That is the nature of women, which is why empowered women drive a better world. Men don't need to be afraid; the train is eager to increase its share of men and women. Nothing is better than being with an intelligent, charming woman and knowing that you can keep your trap shut so she can show you her beauty, grace, and much love. All you need to do is be open, be curious, be willing to experiment, and let the wonder of your life unfold.

# CHAPTER 3
# THE HOW:
# SIMPLE METRICS

Many wealthy people are simple-minded folks. Some of them are like hobbits, minding their own business and only becoming interested in exploring beyond their borders if there is a shortage of ale. Some wealthy folks are like dwarves, intoxicated with hoarding the gold and missing what it represents. A rare bunch brim their minds with opulence and teach the world with their eccentricity and esoteric behaviors. In fantasy stories, these are the wizards.

The kind of wealthy person you want to be is up to you. My job here is to show you how to gain and grow wealth and, along the way, to feel wealthy. Feeling wealthy is to realize the nothingness of money. That is the spirituality of financial empowerment in a nutshell.

Simple rich people are not complicated human beings when it comes to money. They are simple, not simpletons. Simple rich people recognize that building simple habits about money management leads to a luscious, vibrant life. If a simple rich person wants to buy a nice Fender guitar, she researches the market and purchases what she likes. Then she enrolls in a music class. She may choose a group class because she likes the company of other musicians or may prefer a private lesson. She is not oblivious to the financial aspect of this decision.

However, her desire to play the guitar relegates the role of money as only a consideration of affordability. Money spent on learning guitar is a minor reference because she is comfortable with her finances and wants to learn and grow in new dimensions. Wouldn't it be great if more people developed that confidence and poise?

Simple rich people measure their finances and know their financial worth. Simple rich people are diligent and consistent. The oddity is that they spend significantly less time thinking about money than most and rarely worry about it. They continue to look at opportunities to improve their wealth and financial situation constructively. Simple rich people have devised a simple system for how to do this. And learning this system gets you moving and walking toward the State of Z.

The system comprises simple metrics and habits for managing these metrics. Tracking provides early warning signs so the ship doesn't crash into an iceberg. Like any new system, the time it takes in the beginning may seem a bit arduous, but soon enough the habits and the resulting benefits grow on you. You can be flawed in following the system. Old-fashioned grit will be enough.

Simple metrics to manage wealth define your current state and the direction that will influence your future state. Snapshot metrics provide a view of your financials as of that day. Flow metrics anticipate future trends. Calculating both snapshot and flow metrics is simple and learnable. A simple calculator or computer that can do addition and subtraction will do nicely. A ten-year-old boy helping out his mother in Oakland in her business calculates these. An eighty-year-old man watching out for his legacy to his grandkids in Chicago figures these. Calculating metrics is as learnable as brushing teeth or eating cereal. You can do both activities effortlessly, given that you are reading this book at least by choice. If you still need to brush your teeth, let's prioritize that first.

## Snapshot Metrics

The snapshot metrics reflect: A. current monetary resources minus liabilities, B. financial resources available with relative ease (the experts call this liquidity), and C. monies owed to other people and institutions. If you want to sound knowledgeable (and I recommend you do), the first metric is net worth, the second is liquid assets, and the third is good ol' fashioned debt.

Net worth is assets minus liabilities. Assets are something of value that you own, and liabilities are a debt or financial obligation you owe. The most considerable debt for most individuals and households is the mortgage on a primary residence. Other debts include car loans, credit card dues, and student loans. If you have promised to pay someone and need to pay them, that constitutes a liability.

Assets include what you own, either in whole or part. Primary homes, investment properties, vacation homes, investment accounts, cars, cash, stock, and personal property such as jewelry and art qualify as assets. If you have a home with a market value of $300,000 and owe $220,000 to the bank, then the net worth is $80,000 (i.e., $300,000 - $220,000). Net worth paints an honest picture of your financial wealth. Net worth increases when you save or pay down debt or when assets increase in market value. However, the gyrations of the market can erode net worth.

Liquid assets include cash, bank accounts, and stock. These can all be easily liquidated and are available to meet short-term needs and emergencies. It may not be an opportune time to sell stocks in an hour of need, but having liquid money for life's emergencies helps gain and maintain access to Station Z.

The third snapshot metric, debt, measures liabilities. Debt is subtracted from the market value of assets to yield net worth. Monitoring the three metrics provides the foundation of a well-orchestrated financial symphony. Together, these numbers depict how much a person is worth financially unencumbered by liabilities, how much monetary resources are deployable with short notice and the money owed. The rule of thumb is to have a sufficiently positive and growing net worth, liquid assets to cover six months of expenditures for singles or married couples, and one year for parents or those with dependents such as aging parents. Unless the debt is part of an overall risk strategy helping you get on the fast track for significantly greater net worth (such as purchasing real estate investments on leverage or a reasonable student loan to get a college education), the debt objective should be nada. Zero. Nuclear. This simple goal will prevent you from taking excessive loans for homes, cars, and luxuries intended to warp you in a cocoon of stress. And with moderate loans, there will be an incentive to clear out the dues for such matters with zeal and gusto.

The tracking and growth of the three metrics fuels self-reliance. The journey begins with awareness of the current state, followed by a desire to improve personal behaviors and spending habits. For perfectionists with utopian tendencies, and I have found myself on that lonely island sometimes, small incremental steps lead to massive changes over time. For more on this powerful subject, *Atomic Habits* by James Clear is highly recommended reading.

Tracking and measuring snapshot metrics empowers individuals to live their lives per their true calling. Enabling one's calling is not a get-out-of-jail-free card to relieve responsibility but a door to access a greater sense of freedom and live your authentic life. How does tracking three simple metrics set up a path to financial empowerment? It is human behavior to explore avenues to improve our current circumstances. It is also human behavior to let our biases cloud the reality of the situation. The snapshot metrics give you an accurate picture of your financial health. Net worth tells you whether you are under or above water and to what extent you are well above water or surviving with loan sharks under deep debt. The current state of our financials reflects our past behaviors and circumstances, which are helpful as teachers and as a baseline. It is the base camp as you start climbing toward the summit. Though viewing your current state may be an emotional experience, I encourage you to peer into the future and consider the base camp from the top of a summit. Looking down at your base camp, how would you feel about yourself and the journey to liberation?

Debt, another simple but powerful metric, illustrates how much we owe to a third party. Many past great leaders, including America's founding fathers, stressed the need for lower debt. In their experience of building a country of strength, many founding fathers viewed debt as a risk to liberty for the individual and the nation. They viewed public debt with skepticism in political and even moral terms. A profundity from Benjamin Franklin goes, "When you run in debt, you give to another power over your liberty." Thomas Jefferson viewed personal and national debt as threats to the American experiment in self-government. Debt is synonymous with mental and physical stressors. When people indicate money is a stressor, debt is usually a big part of the equation, driving our limited resources into someone else's coffers.

Brandishing all debt as tainted is an old wives' tale. Thoughtfully undertaken debt obligations can lead to significantly improved financial outcomes. There are two rules of thumb that you can apply in your decision-making to take on debt. First, the only debt worth taking on is the one you can pay comfortably without losing sleep. Meeting this condition mitigates any adverse impact on your health and well-being. Second, any debt that helps you better yourself over the long term financially or broaden your exposure and experience is worth taking on.

Real estate investors often leverage debt to drive better financial outcomes with limited upfront investment. Tim, an office manager in a real estate company, invests $50,000 to buy a $200,000 condo.

Tim puts in 25% down to lock in low-interest rates for a thirty-year fixed mortgage. Tim's condo appreciates after five years to $300,000. Though Tim's debt has increased by roughly $150,000, his net worth has increased by approximately $100,000. Tim is wealthier by $100,000. And his $50k investment gave him a 200% cumulative return over just five years! He also benefited from tax provisions that allow homeowners to deduct interest payments. Effective use of debt can turbocharge you to financial freedom faster than simply a 9 to 5 job.

The liquidity metric prepares you with data to develop a rational basis for taking on life risks and assessing your wherewithal for taking on new ventures. The power of deployable resources gives you the boost to enjoy life and not be worried about small unexpected outlays, part and parcel of this journey for all, and makes your stay at Station Z much more protracted.

Anya is a thirty-two-year-old single woman living in Austin, Texas. She has worked full-time for seven years at a financial services company, her first job since completing her MBA. During the first round of layoffs at her company in mid-2022, she became financially conscious about her spending habits and started tracking the three metrics. Her company has since experienced another round of layoffs, and though her job is still safe Anya is open to alternatives and prepared with her financial data.

Anya's net worth is $350k (condominium - $200k, cash - $40k, stock - $50k; 401k - $60k). Her liquidity is $90k (Cash - $40k, Stock - $50k), and debt is $280k (condo - $250k, car - $25k; credit cards - $5k). Recently, a recruiter contacted her to join a small fintech company. The base salary will be roughly the same, but this is an opportunity for Anya to learn the fintech business from the ground up. A higher-growth company may fast-track her career. On the flip side, there is a risk. Changing a job means losing tenure at her current company, and working with a new boss and culture is always risky. Given the current layoffs at her existing company and the opportunity for growth at the new company, Anya is considering this opportunity.

She brings this up while having dinner with her father, an experienced banker. Her dad inquires whether she can take the risk financially if she leaves for this opportunity and things don't work out. Anya's immediate response is "maybe." When she is back at her condominium, Anya starts reviewing the three simple metrics. Anya's net worth is positive, propelled by an increase in the condominium's value. She also had liquid assets worth $90k and debt of $280k. However, she needs more information on her running expenses. Anya has a snapshot of her finances but also needs to understand the trend. She knows her current position via snapshot metrics but needs more data to reveal where her finances are trending. In other words, she needs to know her flow metrics.

### *Flow Metrics*

Flow metrics are the yin to the yang of static snapshot metrics. Snapshot metrics provide your current financial position, and flow metrics indicate the direction and future financial situation. Snapshot metrics tell you a story of where you have reached due to your past behaviors and circumstances. Flow metrics help you predict your future based on your current behaviors and develop clairvoyance to plan your life. It would be misleading to assume you control the future state. However, accurately interpreting trends and willingness to evolve behaviors is an effective antidote to managing life's twists and turns.

Flow metrics comprise monthly expenditures by spending categories and monthly savings. These simple flow metrics depict expenses and the spending categories that constitute these expenditures. Common spending categories are mortgage, grocery, personal care, home repairs, child care, medical, gifts, R&R, pet care, etc. Harnessing the knowledge of these metrics provides insights to reduce wasteful expenditures and highlights key spending areas. These revelations are illuminating because it reflects priorities and interests. In the spirit of innocuous experimentation and frivolity, let these metrics guide you in the journey of self-awareness and willingness to experiment with behaviors that may lead to an evolving you.

Chapters 7 and 8 cover budgeting and spending categories. These chapters detail the mechanics of calculating flow metrics. Table A below summarizes snapshot and flow metrics. In addition to calculating the five metrics, monitoring changes in the metrics provides keen insights. The key to measuring change is subtracting the previous month's figures from the current month's figures. The recommended frequency of calculating these is monthly. Once you have a gauge for calculating these, you can reduce the frequency to quarterly. This recommendation also pares with operating your finances like a business (Chapter 6). A monthly cadence for the first two years is a strong recommendation. After that, you may consider a quarterly cadence. I changed mine to quarterly after ten-plus years of monthly cadence. As you calculate metrics, you will start noticing improvements in other areas of your life, such as your health and relationships. Many of you will like the progress of your metrics so much that it may be difficult at a future point to go to quarterly. After all, positive, upbeat news is better to receive every month than every three months! Personal success is addictive, as is a need to pat yourself on the back! You can put the back scratcher back—your hand will do.

| Metric | Measures | Calculation | Type | Goal |
|---|---|---|---|---|
| Net Worth | Financial health | Assets - Liabilities | Snapshot | Positive & Trending Growth |
| Liquid Assets | Easily accessible assets | Cash + Stocks + Bank Accounts | Snapshot | Positive & Trending Growth |
| Debt | Amount owed to creditors | Home Loans + Car Loans + Credit Cards Balance etc. | Snapshot | Zero (exception for "good" debt that drives long-term personal and financial well-being) |
| Monthly Expenditures | Spending breakdown by category | Categorization & Tracking (Covered in later chapters) | Flow | Mindful & Strategic expenditures |
| Monthly Savings | Saving | Income - Expenses | Flow | Positive & Trending Growth |

Table A. Simple Metrics

## Application of Flow Metrics in Anya's Decision Making

We are back in Anya's world. She had the snapshots of her finances, but she needed the trending metrics. Anya reviews her last six months of monthly expenditures through her credit card and bank statements and can also estimate her savings by reducing her expenses from income from her job. She also categorizes expenses into spend categories such as mortgage, car expenditures, gas, grocery, grooming, home repair, and pet care. Anya benefits from the "malady" of foresight, a formidable trait and a telling sign of her thoughtfulness. While organizing her finances, she recognizes several spending areas where the outlay surprises her. Sunlight, after all, is the best disinfectant and a renewable energy source. Conversely, she also wonders if she could spend more on her grooming and her book collection if she could reduce some of her undesirable expenses. She is now armed with the metrics to evaluate risk, and she puts these metrics on a whiteboard in her office space.

Static Metrics
Net Worth: $350,000
Liquidity: $90,000
Debt: $280,000


Flow Metrics (Based on the last six months)
Monthly Expenditures: $3,500
Monthly Savings: $1,200

The flow metrics provide Anya with a rich perspective of her financial situation. With her monthly expenditures known, Anya knows that if she switches to a new company she can assume a worst-case scenario of not finding a job for six months. She is confident that with her experience and connections she can find a job within six months. For six months, Anya needs $21,000 of emergency money ($3,500 monthly expenditures x 6 months). Reviewing her liquidity details (Cash - $40k, Stocks - $50k), she has sufficient cash that exceeds her expenses for six months. Her Benjamins can support her expenditures for almost twelve months! Now the decision-making is quite simple. She visits her father for dinner that night and shares this information with him. His response, "So what's the downside?" Anya accepted the new role the following day. Before she starts her new role, she opens a bank account, names it the "Twists and Turns Fund," and puts $21k in it.

Let's shift from Austin, TX to Fort Collins, CO. We are at a local business, the Ford's Car Wash, Tom and Betty Ford's business. They started this local car wash ten years ago after Tom and Betty decided to quit their corporate jobs in their mid-thirties and work for themselves. In a moment for the ages, they both gave notice on the same day after they had decided to partner with Betty's brother, who was running two car wash centers of his own. Ten years later, they own two car wash centers with repeat customers and high customer satisfaction and have become a recognizable local business.

Tom and Betty's car wash is called Molly's, after their daughter. Molly is now eighteen and helps with the business. She is pursuing a business degree, and her business experience bolstered her college application. Molly applied to eight colleges, her top choice being Vanderbilt, where her parents met as students. She got accepted at Vanderbilt and the University of Colorado, Boulder, a good school with much lower overall costs ($30,000) than Vanderbilt's $84,000 yearly. Neither school has offered a scholarship, though financial aid is available.

Tom and Betty have high hopes for their daughter, their only child, and would like to explore supporting her dreams of attending Vanderbilt and pursuing a business degree. Being successful business folks, these simple rich people diligently manage their finances and calculate simple metrics with a monthly cadence.

Snapshot metrics for Tom & Betty Ford

I.   Net Worth: $2M

   A.   Business Net Worth - $600k - Not Liquid (Business sale transactions typically can take several months to execute)

   B.   Primary Home - $500k - Not Liquid (Home sale transactions can take several weeks to months to execute

   C.   Investment Home - $200k - Not Liquid (Home sale transactions can take several weeks to months to execute. Their current renters signed a 1-year lease)

D. Retirement Accounts - $300k - Not Liquid (Only available at 59.5. Early withdrawal will trigger penalties)

E. Stocks - $200k - Liquid

F. Cash - $150k - Liquid

G. 529 account (investment account for college) - $50k - Not Liquid

II. Liquidity: $350k (Stock + Cash)

III. Debt: $1.8M

A. Business Debt - $1.4M

B. Primary Home: $150k

C. Investment Home: $250k

IV. Monthly Expenditure (Personal & Business): $40k

V. Monthly Savings: $7.5k (Annual savings: $90k)

Molly's generates positive cash flow. The total four-year expenses for Molly's education at Vanderbilt is $336,000 (84,000 x 4). The Fords can support Molly's first year of college. They are still determining funding for the remaining three years. Though they have liquidity and a business that generates savings, business earnings can be fickle, especially if the economy falters. Car washes are discretionary, and many customers will downgrade to basic service offerings or wash their car themselves.

They initially debate the possibility of paying fully for Molly's four-year college, but doing so would significantly erode savings and rob Molly of the experience to fend for herself. So they meet with Molly and suggest a team effort for Molly's college. Tom & Betty will provide 100% for Molly's first-year education, 80% for Molly's second year, and 50% for Molly's third and fourth years. The total four-year cost to the Fords will be roughly $235,000. Given an estimated $360k savings over the next four years (extrapolating annual $90k savings times 4), 529k of $50k, and current cash of $150k, this should be well within their financial wherewithal. This approach will place the responsibility of $100k on Molly. They appreciate Molly's help at the car wash and offer her a summer job, which will provide her roughly $30k over four years ($7.5k for three months of work). Molly will need to take ~$70k in student loans, but she will only begin to need them in the last semester of the second year.

Applying simple metrics builds the muscles of decision-making and problem-solving, resulting in the north star of spending time at Station Z. A life well spent is often inversely co-related with financial stressors. All of us will face decisions that will create conflict. Knowing your financial health will equip you to tackle high-pressure financial decisions (buying a home, starting a business, paying for college).

Decision-making is not simply a valuable personal trait. It is valued in corporate life as well. Strong and competent decision-making is valuable in any setting because it empowers employees and leaders to make mindful, rational choices that help deliver favorable outcomes. It also makes people adept at analyzing risk and pivoting to alternatives when the expected result does not materialize. The path to financial empowerment also prepares individuals for competencies valued outside their personal life. Wouldn't you want to hire someone who manages their finances and makes ethical, rational, and balanced decisions?

# CHAPTER 4

# BEHAVIORS OF SIMPLICITY

Simple rich people. How would we define simple rich people? Simple rich people come from all races, all religions, all genders. Is there a common defining characteristic that is representative of this group? First, let's break down the "euphemism" in this statement, Simple… Rich…People. The most straightforward word to define is "people." I don't think that is up for debate.

Next, who does "rich" refer to? Rich doesn't simply mean wealthy. One can be wealthy by lots of mechanisms. The least time-consuming solution to being wealthy is to be born one. Wealthy babies wake up in a loving house and a safe city with parents who can provide a few luxuries in addition to (hopefully) love and care. I wish more babies were born into families like that. A positive start in life is a blessing. But "rich" in the context of the title refers to a wealthy state of mind. Many people, such as monks or ascetics, live rich, fulfilling lives without families, iPhones, or computers. If these monks and ascetics are satisfied with their lives, they qualify as rich. For most people however, families, children, school, and work are part of life's rigamarole. We find life's richness more vividly as part of these relationships and the hustle and bustle of life. Money is a necessity for enjoying those pleasures.

Children have never been more expensive to raise. A recent study by the Brookings Institution for the Wall Street Journal found that due to unprecedented inflation rates, parents can expect to spend at least $300,000 raising a child born in 2015 until age 17.[2] Getting old is not getting cheaper either. According to Genworth Financial, in the United States, the national median cost of assisted living facilities in 2021 was $4,500 per month or $54,000 annually.[3]

Add to this a workplace that is increasingly shifting the weight and responsibility of the burden of retirement on the workforce. This statistic is by no means castigating the corporations; they are being responsive to their financial health and the improving longevity demographics of the general population. However, the impact of these trends is lucid. The accountability of financial health has never been more on the individual. With social safety nets evaporating and the nuclear family rising, individuals must add financial well-being to their life skills, and excelling in these provides significant advantages to the individual's quality of life and the richness of experience.

The word "simple" in simple rich people is most nuanced and layered, thereby open to misinterpretation. Simple can often have a negative connotation. Simple, to many, reflects a lack of depth. People are often intrigued by objects, ideas and people that seem complicated. Complexity gives an allure of being challenging, often co-related with attractiveness. Cultures worldwide celebrate victory over challenges as an ideation of a well-lived life.

Yet, simplicity with habits is a cornerstone of rich people leading fulfilling lives. Though it may seem counterintuitive in our hyper-commercialized social media-throbbing, constantly chaotic competition-crazed culture, simple patterns with money drive simple rich people to live their lives on their terms and manage life's complexities with empathy and kindness toward themselves and others. The simplicity of money management allows simple rich people to navigate life's hurdles with courage and compassion and not antipathy toward the circumstances and people that are so often the incubators.

No book can capture all the behaviors and habits of simplicity. Many simple practices have a history of origins in cultures, religions, and societies in response to the age-old question of the meaning of life or to drive societal progress. Others have arisen out of the ingenuity of individuals laboring through a way to solve problems. Some simple behaviors are often breakthroughs, but many more times result from incremental improvements over time, followed by an aha moment, "the breakthrough." It is a token of self-awareness of individuals and society to improve their lives and those of their loved ones. Simple habits have passed from generation to generation via word of mouth, cultural acceptances, and books. I share some of these as examples and encourage you on this journey to build your own.

When you create, you will likely share. In that way, you mirror the teachers on the train who teach others to start walking, moving, and helping them on their way to Station Z. You will often note that simple rich people are often solving for time and convenience, which allows them to focus on what matters to them. They are okay with paying money for new experiences and partaking in and learning from the complexity of life, which they engage with relentlessly and often with an insatiable curiosity. And the confidence and poise with which simple rich people face lives starts with the simplicity of their habits. A simple routine can have a far-reaching impact by creating space and decluttering energy. An example of the positive effects of a simple habit follows.

Simple Habit - Finish Leftover Food at Home
Before Cooking New Dishes

What does it accomplish?

- Reduces waste of food
- Saves time to cook and clean utensils
- Reduces grocery bills
- Reduces trips to grocery stores
- Fosters creativity and problem-solving in cooking
- Increases consciousness of cooking, reducing leftovers
- preparing food to satiate present hunger
- The quality-of-life improvement for women

A simple habit of first finishing up leftovers (assuming they are not spoilt, of course) has far-reaching consequences, not on saving money on groceries but by saving time for cooking and cleaning utensils and shopping at grocery stores. And because it's far too easy to make another thing, especially with the abundance of food in most of the developed world, working with a limitation forces our brains to devise creative solutions for meal preparation. As an example, let's say a family of four has leftover stew. But the leftover stew would feed only two. The family could cut fruits instead of creating a meal to fill the gap. Not only do fruits constitute a healthy meal, but cutting fruits is not time consuming. Additionally, this simple habit increases consciousness of food preparation and reduces waste in households and societies.

This simple habit also triggers a far-reaching social change. It improves the quality of life for women, who even now bear the brunt of cooking and housework. Though men contribute more in the house, and many men are rising to this challenge, a woman's life is still more chaotic and burdensome. And providing food for the family is still seen by most as a woman's job. Reducing direct and indirect activities to support cooking frees the woman to care for her and her family's needs. She can watch television, get a nice massage, or sleep. She may also be available for creative pursuits, whether sports, music, theater, singing, or just some free time if she gets a break from handling the frying pan. All the benefits above accrue because of the simple habit of consuming leftovers before making another meal.

Let's dig into a few more simple habits that simple rich people follow to make their lives richer, metaphorically and literally. These habits are for your guidance, not for blind obedience. Follow 'em, tweak 'em, twist 'em. Experiment relentlessly with callous confidence. When it clicks, you'll know. The benefits are categorized into three broad buckets: money savings, time savings, and quality of life improvements.

| Habit | Money | Time | Quality of Life |
|---|---|---|---|
| Make a list at home prior to grocery shopping | Avoids duplicate/ unnecessary buys<br><br>Preparing a list at home focuses you in a distraction-free zone on necessities and avoids random purchases.<br><br>Research indicates grocery lists can reduce food expenses by 25-30% | Saves time in the grocery store by avoiding unnecessary dawdling<br><br>Making a grocery list may drive the selection of the grocery store and consolidate trips to various grocery stores<br><br>Fewer trips to the grocery store | May help with meal planning<br><br>Improve grocery shopping experience |

| | | | |
|---|---|---|---|
| **Paying with cash (where possible)** | Merchants avoid credit card fees and may give a discount. | Unless planned in advance, may mean more trips to ATM machines.<br><br>The friction in the process may create an incentive to shop less. | Creates financial discipline with purchasing only what you can afford |
| **Making extra payments on mortgage** | Reduces interest paid on loans<br><br>Allocates money to necessary expenditures, thereby reduces frivolous expenditures | Saves time off mortgage to allow for pursuing other meaningful life goals that often get delayed / never get started because of financial responsibilities | Less stress on account of staying ahead on mortgage payments<br><br>Feeling of levity and freedom on account of paying off mortgage early |

Let's take the example of Charlie Shin, who worked in a software company. Charlie, 40, and his wife Kim, 38, are simple rich people. Married fourteen years with two kids, Myrah, 8, and Alex, 1, their lives underwent a significant transformation during Covid. Managing work while taking care of virtual school and homework of the eight-year-old and taking care of the one-year-old without any nanny created immense stress for the family and even brought their marriage to teeters. The yelling increased in their home, adding tension to each other and their kids.

Kim was working in the county, and her workload increased as her team supported the county on the financial impact of an ever-changing Covid environment. Though Charlie was competent in his field, managing Covid with two young kids took a toll on his mental health, and he got a new boss who was insensitive to his family situation. The company's performance was mediocre, and Charlie started entertaining other offers. But there were two critical approaches to how Charlie reviewed his options vs. many others who would have been in the same position.

Charlie knew his financial position. His debt situation was manageable, even if he and his wife had no jobs. Though he was not pleased with his boss's demeanor, he was also not overly anxious about this situation. Six months before he left his current job for a better opportunity, Charlie started to take better care of himself. He started exercising regularly, meditating more often, spending quality time with his kids, and socializing more as the risk from Covid decreased. These changes were incremental, but slowly and steadily, Charlie started feeling better. He got three job offers, one from a consulting company, another from a smaller technology company, and a third from his previous employer. He joined his previous employer because of the company culture and business stability. Charlie had learned from his earlier experience that culture is priceless. And he was able to earn more money and landed a promotional opportunity. As I write this, Charlie has been in the role for one year, and as he looks back, he is satisfied with his decision. He does well in his job, reporting to a leader whom he respects, works with a team that he feels connected to, and leads key projects.

Charlie's story accentuates the relationship between our finances and decision-making. Simple rich people do not let others bully them. They build a life with dignity and respect, where they call the shots. Charlie did not just hop at the first job he got. He also did not switch to another job for just money. Though money was a consideration in his decision, the critical criteria for him were the people he would work with, his role, and the culture he would be part of. His decision was also not based on immediate gratification but on where he would enjoy the journey, his long-term prospects, and the organization's business projections. Not title, not money, but long-term value for him. Charlie negotiated well and made more money than before, and though money was a consideration, his decision-making reflected his true priorities and physical and mental well-being. Charlie's state of mind was at Station Z, where he could see longer and broader than most people in a similar situation. Short-term money implications did not hamstring him. If Charlie had not known his money situation, he would likely have made an alternative decision. He could have stayed at the same job and worked harder for an unappreciative boss. He could have switched to an opportunity that came his way right away or may have shown desperation to move to his previous company, which would have resulted in neither the title nor the money he deserved and received. By going slow, exploring his options, and deliberating on the long-term implications of his decisions, Charlie made the choice that he believed would align with his goals and values.

Simple rich people regard wealth as a reflection of growth and progress. Subsequently, simple rich people inculcate habits that drive self-growth. Many of these are well documented in Thomas C. Corley's work. Thomas Corley spent many years studying self-made millionaires and gathered his insights in several books, including *Change Your Habits, Change Your Life*. Corley's insights reflect a yearning desire by self-made rich people to better themselves by reading, exercising, socializing, and goal setting. And what's profound is not just the activities being performed but the high level of self-awareness and intentionality.

For example, millionaires in Corley's research focus on reading biographies of successful people, personal development, and history books. They intentionally focus reading on subjects to learn and grow themselves. They socialize with people whom they consider successful and who, similar to them, are interested in learning and developing themselves. They volunteer because it builds their character, provides them with a sense of gratitude, and they meet people with similar outlooks. They recognize their most prized resource is themselves, so they invest in their physical and mental well-being. They sleep at least seven hours a day, exercise regularly, get up early, and enhance their self-awareness to monitor and actively foster positive thoughts. They practice these habits consistently. Consistently does not mean 100%; it means not giving up and trying to improve habits' consistency. And, yes, they don't give up on themselves. Like all of us, they have bad days and worse days. But they know it's just another day, and their life is a journey filled with all kinds of days — sunny, cloudy, foggy, and windy. Some days they take significant strides, while others days might be just a stroll, and some days they take cover. But the journey is always afoot.

Most habits that simple rich people strive for don't cost much, and many are available for free. Where there is an outlay of cash, the benefits are outweighed in the long term and often add to significant buying power. It's a gift to yourself that keeps on giving. Exercising can be done in a gym (a reasonable quality establishment is not expensive). A walk, run, or playing a sport does nicely also. Books can be procured from a library (after all, your tax dollars fund it). If you buy them, books are a wise investment, not just because it encourages us to read more. It's also an effective way to nurture successful, intelligent kids. Waking up early doesn't cost a dime. Creating a sleeping routine infused with relaxing music, nighttime reading, and decluttering the brain is not costly. Even when an outlay is involved, simple rich people do not ponder what they can afford. They happily invest in buying a quality mattress. A quality mattress is like buying good shoes. Good quality sleep makes people feel better in their waking hours, and it elongates life, just like good quality shoes help reduce the wear and tear of feet and legs.

The other benefit of many of these habits is time savings. Intentional practices consume time, but in doing so they prevent time from being taken away unintentionally by unproductive activities to our goals and quality of life. The distinction is a pivotal one in how life turns out.

There is quite another evolutionary aspect to the creation of habits. Human beings, being the only species known to us, have a conscious choice to create a habit. The deer does not try to wake up at a particular time. The lion does not fast because it will build self-discipline. The monkey does not strive to be a better listener because she aspires to be a monk. And the wolf does not practice oratory so that one day he can succeed the lion as the jungle king. Animal behavior emanates primarily from instinct and genetics. However, humans have a distinct choice in how we spend our time.

How our lives turn out is a reflection of our behaviors. And our behaviors are governed by habits. Over 40% of what we do is habitual. Dr. Wendy Wood, a psychologist at the University of Southern California's Habit Lab, found that an estimated 43% of daily activities were done habitually, during which study participants were thinking of something else.[4]

Time spent on habits can be divided into three buckets: time we practice developing productive habits consciously (roughly 5% of the time), time spent in habits that do not serve us well, or unproductive habits, and the rest of it. The first bucket is the only one where we are present or gaining presence in the moment, which benefits us now and in our future state. Productive habits generate positive well-being, either physical or mental, in the long term and the moment. Such habits would be exercise, meditation, and having dinner at the dinner table with family.

The second bucket is primarily a state of stupor, a thriving ground for unproductive habits. Unproductive habits create adverse long-term well-being, even if they feel good. Smoking, drugs, alcohol, snacking late at night, and mindlessly watching television are frequent offenders. We may have some self-awareness in this state, but to continue with such negative habits, we silence or mitigate our self-awareness. Self-awareness is the most effective antidote to breaking unproductive habits. Self-awareness communicates to our mind and body that doing nothing is a better alternative than unnecessary motions.

The third bucket of time-consuming habits is automated mechanisms to support our sustenance. Sustaining practices are those we need for the daily running of our lives. Examples are driving to and from work, putting a security alarm on before leaving home, tying shoelaces, and brushing our teeth.

Habits are formed as a channel for human growth. A habit is a program that automates our behavior. The more we automate, the more we can explore, learn, and conquer new habits.

In 1911, the mathematician Alfred North Whitehead wrote, "It is a profoundly erroneous truism that we should cultivate the habit of thinking of what we are doing. The precise opposite is the case. Civilization advances by extending the number of important operations we can perform without thinking about them." If life was a video game, the expertise level of habits is an area indicative of skill.

Self-awareness and conscious attention to personal growth are the seeds for developing productive habits. All habits that you are consciously creating are effective habits. Most people develop habits to better themselves or their lives. Eventually, they may use or plan to use behaviors for goals that may be considered nefarious or socially undesirable. Adolf Hitler was said to practice oratory and used his superior oratory skills for a terrible purpose. The merit of the skills, like science, was still objective, with its application being the responsibility of the doer. Superior oratory skills are a productive habit for the individual, though used for a heinous application by Hitler. The salient point here is that people drive conscious decision-making intending to grow themselves. Effort is a required ingredient in the potion for self-growth. People strive consciously for discipline in exercising by inculcating productive habits. You will hardly meet someone who claims they have a couple of glasses of wine after dinner daily because they consider this habit essential to their growth. It is also unlikely to find someone making a conscious effort to sit in front of the television for two hours daily.

Simple rich people realize the power of habits and focus on consciously developing habits that bring them closer to a financially empowered state. Habits are consciously prioritized for monitoring finances, creating budgets, saving money, and reviewing opportunities to improve financial outcomes. Many simple rich people welcome being replaced by a computer for savings habits such as automatic 401k deduction, automatic contribution to retirement accounts, college funds, etc. They hire the service where they feel better served by using an expert's help, such as an investment or tax expert. Often, such qualified help comes from within their social network. The rich help other rich people. It's a resourceful club to be a part of.

Simple rich people automate simple behaviors that promote their financial goals. This frees up their time to focus on what matters most. Time is money. Simple rich people realize that being at the station of Z does not mean stagnation. It is a continuous state of growth. Money is always necessary but is just not a source of stress. Simple rich people take pride in money management.

Let's take an example of the Smiths, a San Francisco couple who recently celebrated their twentieth anniversary. Nicole and Alan are part of the large swath of middle management with an arduous job of managing people and reporting to their upper management. Alan is in finance, and Nicole is in accounting. They have not inherited any money from their parents and had humble beginnings. Given their finance & accounting backgrounds, they both leaned conservative regarding savings, and early on in their marriage they were careful with their expenditures. Alan maxed his 401k contributions from the beginning of his career, with Nicole following suit shortly. Their companies did

401k matching, and both have automatic 401k contributions to save and take advantage of pre-tax deductions. This was hassle-free habit #1 toward automatic savings.

Ten years ago, Nicole & Alan started Habit # 2 and automated it from the start, monthly deductions toward a low-cost investing service account. Many are available in the market, such as Betterment, Wealthfront, Vanguard, etc. These offerings are of great value as they charge low expense ratios for managing your accounts tied to your risk profile. The "fill it, shut it, forget it" approach is time efficient and yields tax savings through tax harvesting strategies.[5] These companies leverage tax harvesting strategies, which essentially means they sell underperforming stocks that are losing money to offset capital gains and investments that have appreciated, subsequently reducing tax burden for the investors.

Five years ago, Nicole & Alan signed up for a Big Hairy Audacious Goal (BHAG), which is to retire from their jobs in another ten years, i.e., five years from their current state and just when they would be turning the corner beyond fifty. To support their BHAG, they hired a reputable investing firm. They patiently understood the firm's capabilities, did reference checks, and reviewed its long-term performance. This firm also provides financial planning services to help achieve their bold aspirations. For Habit #3, they set aside savings of a target amount of money that would then go into the investment pool managed by investment professionals.

Simple rich people recognize the power of habits and that small changes lead to significant outcomes. Most people can apply the habits that Alan and Nicole developed. They don't have any advantages over a typical person, and they don't have access to inherited money or any unique resources that are only available to them. Alan and Nicole are working Americans who applied these habits consistently and diligently to meet their financial freedom goal and build a happy and productive life for themselves.

## Assignment

The effort is a precursor to change. Please take a break from reading, and create your BHAG.

Here are a few helpful tips:

- Think Big.
- It can be Hairy. The road to success is tortuous, winding, and bumpy.
- Be Bold. It ain't big enough if it ain't tickling you in the bones.
- Be specific. Close your eyes and feel your accomplishments.

# CHAPTER 5

# SAVE TO INVEST

Save to invest is a vigorous and assertive savings strategy that links the perceived passivity of savings to the proactive action of investing. For many, saving money conjures up thoughts and feelings tied to scarcity or a limiting feeling that inhibits behaviors or wants, not entirely positive emotions. When corporate leaders talk about savings or cutting back, employees commonly view that as job-threatening or job-limiting. Alternatively, investing is viewed as growth and has a positive association with it. Investors are seen as competent money managers, savers as frugal and cheap.

There is more to the save-to-invest philosophy than changing the perception with a play of words. Linking savings with investing infuses purpose and delivers vastly improved tangible results for the investor portfolio. The saver and investor gains purpose-driven resilience to progress when facing headwinds, and a sound investing strategy takes advantage of economic tailwinds over the long term.

The foundation of an aggressive investment strategy rests on a strong defensive position. In life, as in sports, a strong defense is the hallmark of teams that deliver strong results. A strong defense frees the offensive lineup to go full throttle. The first step in the save-to-invest strategy is to build that defense to protect your way of life via the power of your savings. This means building an emergency fund of twelve months of savings. An emergency fund of six months of savings may be sufficient for individuals or households without children. This savings pile should be in bank accounts, typically in a money market or savings account that generates bank interest. The key takeaway is for the funds to be easily accessible. This pile of money is earmarked only for emergencies.

The chapter on budgeting will show you how to accurately estimate the emergency fund. As expenses change with life events such as marriage or kids, following the budgeting process will guide you to adjust the emergency fund. Married couples will typically have greater expenditures as the family grows, and emergency funds should be adjusted accordingly to accommodate their changing life scenarios. A periodic process of budgeting helps to create a target for an emergency fund that assures its users of its efficacy. As and when these resources are depleted to meet emergency needs, future savings should be prioritized to fill up these coffers.

Once the target for the emergency fund is met, it is time to execute the next phase of the save to invest strategy by prioritizing investing. Every dollar saved after the emergency fund should be deployed through 401k retirement plans, stocks investments, rental properties, and other investment channels. Robo-investing options such as Wealthfront and Betterment are easy to set up and simplify and automate the process of investing. As of the writing of this book, both portals charge 0.25% for their investments, making it an economical option for investors. Over the last few years, investment access has been democratized, and sites such as Yieldstreet, Arrived, and Masterworks allow individual investors to conveniently invest in real estate and art to diversify their investment portfolio. Exchange-traded funds and mutual funds can also be conveniently purchased via online trading portals such as E-Trade, Ameritrade, and a plethora of others to ensure every dollar after the emergency fund is invested.

There are many books on investment strategies written by financial gurus. As an additive, I would recommend reading the annual reports of Berkshire Hathaway, which are available for free on the Berkshire Hathaway website. Written by Mr. Warren Buffett, these are insightful and entertaining to read. Mr. Buffett provides a good foundation for assessing value and ingrains his long-term view essential for success in any sustainable investment strategy.

No single investment strategy is a surefire winner. However, there are strategies on a continuum from simple to complex to grow your money. Simplicity and complexity are relative terms; to create a more objective and personalized feel, practitioners can apply the TMV framework discussed in the next chapter to assess a few investment strategies. It would be prudent to share certain principles that have been tested over a long period of time. Many readers may find these obvious, but I am bringing these up for the benefit of everyone and to give a boost to all readers for why the strategy of saving to invest is a pragmatic and effective strategy to create wealth.

First, cash is the most effective asset for life's emergencies and running the business of life. However, it is not a good asset to hold in excess of these needs. Inflation reduces the purchasing power of cash over time. Inflation means that the price of goods and services increases. Whether it is the cost of bread or a house, time discounts the cash value. Holding cash also deprives the opportunity to invest in alternative assets that have historically grown at rates beyond inflation. Saving $10,000 cash in a checking account in 1992 would still be $10,000 in absolute terms thirty years later. In real value, as the price of goods and services has increased during this time, the value of $10,000 will be a lot less. With an annual average inflation of 2.5%, the purchasing power of $10,000 has been reduced by more than 50%! If you were to buy the same products in 1992 and 2022 exactly, they would cost you $10,000 and $4,858, respectively. Because of inflation, holding cash beyond regular needs and emergencies will reduce your purchasing power. You can play around with other numbers and years by leveraging the inflation calculator at westegg.com.

Second, there are investing alternatives to holding cash that have yielded returns historically exceeding inflation and subsequently grown purchasing power. Some of these techniques are so simple that after a fifteen-minute setup with an online brokerage firm, you can simply automate the investing process and marvel at how your wealth grows over time. Becoming rich has never been so tactically simple. You can sip the Mai-tai on a sunny Friday afternoon and let the computers do the work!

One of the simplest ways is to invest in the S&P 500, an index fund that includes five hundred of the largest US companies. The S&P includes companies that are leaders in sectors such as Technology (Adobe, Apple, Microsoft, Nvidia, Salesforce), Retail (Amazon, Costco, eBay), Pharmaceuticals (Merck, Pfizer), Financial Products (Bank of America, Citigroup), Heavy Manufacturing (Caterpillar), Medical Devices (Stryker, Intuitive Surgical), Consumer Goods (PepsiCo, Coca Cola), and many other sectors that form the backbone of capitalism. With investments in the S&P 500, you are not just a consumer but also an investor sharing the gains in economic prosperity. The average S&P 500 return over the last thirty years was 9.89%. An investment of $10,000 invested in 1992 and held off until 2022 with dividends reinvested would result in a pile of stock worth more than $170,000. All you had to do was save to invest and then just let it grow. There have been economic downturns during this period, including the 2001 dot com bust and the Great Recession of 2008. There have been years when the stock returns have been negative. However, a long-term investing strategy of buy and hold in 500 of the largest US companies have yielded strong returns while adding diversification to your portfolio.

Third, with the advent of technology, systematic democratization has broadened the accessibility of investment opportunities. Your friendly neighborhood plumber might have a more impressive portfolio than a business executive. She may have investments in art, real estate, treasury bonds, ETFs, and commodities, making her portfolio more diversified than an executive with compensation heavily tilted to stocks. An increasing number of legitimate portals are opening up opportunities to all of us common folk. Crowdstreet, Yielstreet, Arrived, and Masterworks are some of the leading reputable platforms.

Fourth, invest in yourself. This is the most important investment. An investment of your money and, more importantly, time will yield more impressive results than any other. If there is only one golden rule from this work, it is to "invest in self." Investing in the self is investing in your growth and development. If you want to learn to sing, take a singing class. If you want to learn about fishing, plan a trip to a nearby lake. If you want to learn martial arts, take a class and go to martial arts festivals. Be where the action is for your growth, and spend your resources to be part of the action.

Fifth, avoid the noise. Stay focused on investing in yourself. As you invest in yourself, wealth will simply be a byproduct. On the way, you will come across plenty of naysayers and opportunities to divert your attention. And life's happenings will interfere. Your job is to stay focused and tackle life's circumstances in a mature way. True liberty is the reward to those who can meet those demands. But you will often have to say no or find another way to alleviate those asks. You are not telling the people no but rather saying yes to opportunities and possibilities that provide meaning to your life.

Sixth, when investing, fit the investments into your life, not the other way round. You should select investments based on your interests and hobbies. If you love going to museums, art investments may be a good fit. If your interests lie with baseball and trading cards, invest accordingly. If you don't want to spend any time in investments, simply invest in index funds, and Fuhgeddaboudit. Life is good—next challenge.

Seventh, experiment with your investing strategy. Initially, do not dabble too deep. Go slow and steady. Invest a bit, understand the business models, and then you can go deeper if those investments pique your interest. Or limit your losses if you don't believe the investments are meeting your requirements. Experimenting, evaluating, and pivoting are as key to investing as they are to living a good life. I once dabbled a small investment amount with gold and silver after reading a book, and the investments did not do as well. I have not sold my stake but did not add any further assets in those categories.

Finally, connect with people and books. People are the source of investments and ideas. Build a meaningful connection, and you will be leaving an indelibly positive mark. Books have more wealth than could be fathomed in a hundred lifetimes. Reading is a gift that keeps on giving. Recently, I went to the Christiansborg palace in Copenhagen and perused through the Royal family's library. The library hosts the Royal Family's largest collection of Danish and international works, many thousands, including Hans Christian Andersen's fairy tales, the only book I had read in the collection. I felt like a curious little boy finding a whole new magical world that cold rainy day in Copenhagen. Kings of the past considered these useful for governing large empires, and there are immense pearls of wisdom ingrained in the vast bodies of oceans of knowledge accessible through books.

### How to Save

In the previous section, we discussed a growth strategy that funnels savings to investments. The bottom of the funnel is constrained by the savings, which flow through it from the top of the funnel. Savings increase by spending consciously on people and experiences that help you grow and be happy and reducing wasteful expenditures, often associated with noise in our environments and cancerous wants.

Behaviors that reflect conscious spending and habitual savings align with financial well-being. Your approach to making purchasing decisions drives spending and the resulting savings. Take a few minutes and contemplate the following questions. Are most of your purchases planned or spur of the moment? Do you typically purchase goods and services that you need or things you desire or want? Do you typically use the goods and services that you purchase? Do some of your friends or relatives have different purchasing behaviors from yours? Do you see any patterns of satisfaction and well-being correlated with people you know and their spending behaviors?

There is a common thread of needs versus wants in the questions above that underlies spending behaviors and habits and the resulting savings outcomes. Needs versus wants represents a simple concept. When mastered, you are well on your way to being an effective saver. Basically, you should buy the goods and services you need and wait to buy those that you want until you can afford to make the purchases, making sure they're within the parameters you have set for your planned expenditures per the budgeting process.

The line between needs and wants can be blurry though. A simple framework in this chapter will train you to discern the difference. Many, if not most purchases, fall in the wants category, such as the next version of the iPhone when you have a functioning smartphone available. Interestingly, while we spend our resources satisfying our never-ending wants, some of our needs go unmet. Decluttering our purchases to weed out those arising out of unnecessary wants creates space and allows for discovering additional needs that are striving for our time and money. For example, a new skill that is becoming a need that gets you an internship at that social media company you so covet. Or, healthy organic fruits and vegetables that would meet your nutrition needs and would be far cheaper than the cost of vitamins and medicines. And tastier too.

Understanding the distinction between needs and wants and applying this knowledge to purchasing behaviors is a precursor to effectively managing spending. Needs are basic things we need to live and function. Food is a need. Shelter is a need. Clothing is a need. Even though clothing is a need, designer clothes are not a need. Similarly, healthy food is a need to fuel our body and brain. Healthy food stocked in a fridge will do nicely. Going to Denny's for late night snacking on eggs and that juicy burger is a want.

Counterintuitively, there may also be needs that are unfulfilled in spite of money being spent to procure them. A shortage in intake of healthy foods with necessary minerals and vitamins may be a fairly common example. Even though there may be significant purchases of processed food or fast food, it may not be providing nutrients that a higher quality food would provide.

The needs vs. wants classification can be blurry. The needs vs. wants framework on the next page helps you categorize them in the right bucket. There is nothing wrong with buying something you don't really need as long as you have budgeted for it and can actually afford it. The intent is not to avoid purchases but to increase purchasing consciousness and drive decision-making that aligns with your financial growth.

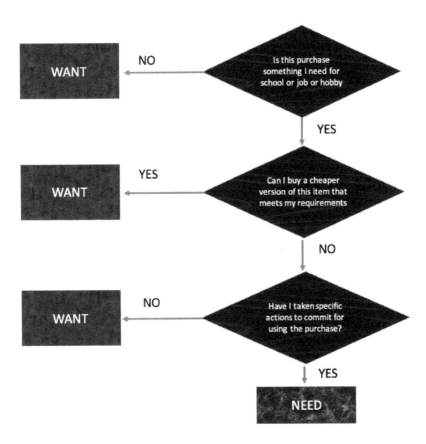

This simple framework can be applied instantaneously and in any setting. The first question focuses on whether the purchase supports a relevant focus category such as a job, school, or a hobby. Hobbies broaden the qualification scope, and encourage practitioners to broaden skills, and take up new activities. If the answer is affirmative, the next question inquires whether there is a more cost-effective substitute. Finally, the last question pertains to the urgency of the purchase and increases the likelihood that the purchase will be put to the intended use. Often, people make purchases thinking of a future project or activity they plan to undertake. For example, someone may buy a set of ski gear assuming they will pursue this activity. Purchasing a season ticket at a ski park could be considered a commitment to taking up skiing, justifying the purchases; a ski rental should be first considered for first-timers to evaluate the sport before making a big commitment.

Next, we will illustrate how to apply this framework. Picasso, an electrician, loved painting as a kid and intends to practice at home after work. After shopping on a few online sites, Picasso orders a paint set from eBay. In this case, the paint set qualifies as a need. For Picasso, painting is a hobby. He has shopped for the paint set that met his needs and purchased a competitively priced quality paint set.

A college student, Erika is a Swiftie interested in attending the Eras tour. This is a want as it does not support work, school, or a hobby. However, if Erika can afford it and is within her budget, she should go. I hear Taylor Swift's concerts are quite a spectacle.

Effective personal finance management may seem much more complex and complicated than simply managing spending habits. Still, the fundamental concept of not spending your money on things you don't need is vital to grasp, as well as understanding that buying material things is not likely to give you happiness as portrayed in the media.

Let's examine two scenarios to see how relatively small amounts of money can add to differing outcomes over time. Nicole gets an allowance of $25 per week. Her parents cover all her necessary expenses, such as food, shelter, and clothing, so the allowance is at her discretion. When she gets her allowance on Fridays, she immediately heads off to the mall and buys makeup and clothes. Any leftover money is fodder for sodas and snacks. She saves only when she wants to buy something that costs more than $25, but her typically weekly ritual is to spend all of it.

Nicole continues to receive this allowance for three years before getting a part-time job. During this time, Nicole does not save any money. An allowance of $25 does not seem like a lot of money, but within three years she has received a total of $3,900. That's enough money to buy a decent used car, but not with Nicole's spending habits.

Like Nicole, her friend Maria receives a weekly allowance of $25. Unlike Nicole, Maria spends only a portion of her allowance and saves the rest in a savings account. Her savings vary, but on average she saves $15 weekly. Because Maria is disciplined at savings, when she really desires a purchase and its affordable, she doesn't have to wait too long. For example, she wanted to buy a bicycle to get around quickly to her classes without waiting for public transportation, which she did. This savings pattern continues for three years until she gets a part-time job. Within the same three-year period, Maris has saved $2,340, and with a 1% interest rate, Maria is a proud owner of a $2,375 savings account.

Habits that reduce unnecessary spending and increase savings have huge payoffs. For example, a person making $100,000 and contributing 15% every year in the stock market with a return of 6% in line with historical returns would have $200,000 after ten years and $1M after twenty-seven years. Even a relatively small amount of money can accumulate with the magic of compound interest. This simple act of savings consistently is not all that common. Of the 250 million adults in the United States, only 5%, roughly 11 million, are millionaires.

## Pervasive Advertising

Capitalism has provided far-reaching benefits. It has helped reduce significant poverty over the last one hundred years, promoted greater economic well-being, and has brought people from different backgrounds together, resulting in greater inclusivity and connectivity. While acknowledging the positives of a system that encourages innovation and sales, capitalism, especially in its current state, promotes a pervasive and intrusive sales culture. The tip of the spear is advertising, targeting consumers incessantly and pervasively with the intent to increase consumer spending. Individuals and their data are highly valuable and intriguing to advertisers. Certain groups are more attractive to advertisers. If you are a teenager, you are especially targeted for disposable income, which means you have the money you can spend without worrying that you won't be able to pay your mortgage or other expenditures adults typically prioritize.

Advertisers are incentivized to increase your spending and don't want you to know they are trying so hard. If you are going to take control of your money and spending, you need to know marketers are always messaging you, even when you do not realize it. What types of messages are they communicating? Advertisers want you to feel that you will need their product to be popular or that a certain product will make you cool or make your life much better than it is now.

They use many different types of advertising to influence you to buy certain clothes, buy certain types of cars, and attend certain types of events. It's not always easy to spot an attempt at getting you to buy something. Advertising is often subtle and sneaky and will be placed beyond the obvious spots in television and radio commercials. You will consciously and subconsciously be targeted for advertising when driving your car, casually walking with a friend, or doing daily chores. Pay attention the next time you go to a mall, a department store, or are just perusing through the streets. You will encounter advertising for products and services across various mediums. Videos playing on screens overhead. Sign for a realtor on the bench of a bus stop. A larger-than-life cut-out at your grocery store for purchasing a six-set red wine. Signs at the movie theater entrance show friends enjoying a five-gallon drink and an equivalently sized popcorn, enough for a dinner for two giraffes. The groups of friends are smiling and happy — who wouldn't be after a high-calorie snack? It's quite another matter that if you follow suit and make a similar purchase, your breath will stink, feel bloated, and none the wiser, since you paid $8 for popcorn that the movie theater made for a dollar.

Then there are the movie placements during the movies, which have multiplied as well. In the 1960s, James Bond films had an average of about five product placements per film. By the 2010s, an average Bond film featured around thirty product placements per film, ranging from alcohols to cars to laptops – a sixfold increase![6] You are watching the movie, and the advertisers are watching your wallet and stealthily emptying it! Wake up, Watson, and smell the fat in the popcorn!

Why is being aware of ubiquitous advertising messages targeted at you important? To generate savings, you need to manage your spending. Recognizing the efforts targeted at you to spend money on products and services that you may not need or use much prepares you to mitigate the impact of outside forces driving your decisions. Companies invest significant resources to better understand what packaging to put products in, the color, texture so people notice and consider buying it. There is nothing wrong with companies advertising and messaging consumers, but you need to be aware what the purpose of advertising is, and when you make purchasing decisions, make sure they are based on your intrinsic needs.

Much of advertising is focused on driving an action from the targeted audience. It could be to garner your vote on a proposition, vote for a political candidate, or nudge you toward a purchasing decision now or in the future. Impulse buying is when you buy something you did not plan to buy and later realize that you did not need. Impulse buying can become an issue when it turns into compulsive shopping or when it leads to unintended purchases that hamper your financial plans. Compulsive shoppers often get a rush from shopping, and this rush is followed by a feeling of guilt or depression, similar to a smoker who is trying to quit or a dieter that first eats many scoops of ice cream then feels guilty and depressed.

In case you feel like you are a compulsive shopper, please reach out to a guidance counselor or a therapist. There are many resources available on the internet via a simple Google search. Chances are that you are not a compulsive shopper, but we have all been participants in impulse purchases. The point is not to beat yourself for impulse shopping but to accept these as a learning experience and reduce such incidents.

## Beat It, Impulse Buying!

Simple effective strategies can reduce impulse buying and reduce your spending. Budgeting, covered in detail later in this book, is a simple effective strategy for planning and tracking your expenditures. The swashbuckling budgeter sets spend targets by category, tracks spend against the targets, develops a fact-based understanding of spend patterns, and tweaks habits to improve financial outcomes.

Another effective way is to automate systematic decision-making that delivers savings. For example, automatic 401k deductions from your paycheck saves money for retirement, reduces your tax burden, and many organizations match 401k contribution providing a very handsome return on investment. 529 plans for college allow for automatic deduction from bank accounts and allow for tax benefits on the growth of investments while providing a growing pool for college expenditures. Investment portals allow automatic deductions from bank accounts to invest in mutual funds and ETFs. Setting up any of these automated mechanisms takes a few minutes. However, some prior due diligence is recommended to understand the players and gain an understanding of the products and services. Slowly and steadily, these investments grow and help you reach the State of Z. While you traverse the complexities of life with increased responsibilities, your nest egg is growing. Contributing such savings grows your gold and reduces the monies that otherwise you may spend on expenses that will take away from your investments. A simple, effective way to spend less on discretionary expenditures is to have less surplus money. Having fewer disposable resources acts as a constraint and fosters creativity.

Budgeting and automated savings are effective planning and investing strategies that generate savings and wealth. But, for most of us, learning how to manage our emotions in the moment is also critical to generating savings. Buyer's remorse is more common than we would think and happens after small and big ticket items purchases. It may include the yellow dress that lost its shine in our living room, the antique furniture that seems out of place after delivery, the eighty-five-inch OLED television that covers half the living room, that red sports car that screams mid-life crisis, or that home, the cornerstone of the American dream. With the complicated feelings from the daily stress, anxieties, and hopes, the incessant messaging from the many commercials and stores around us can seem like a soothing balm. And then there is the peer pressure. However, there is a very simple time intervention strategy to avoid impulse buying. You can apply this strategy to other facets of your life to build positive and disrupt negative habits. The time intervention strategy will reduce impulse buying immediately without any further training or changes you need to make. You do not need to be thinner, smarter, or taller for these. You do not need to change anything about yourself to implement these rules. You can effectively use these in the present moment. The effect is positive, impactful, and immediate.

The simple time intervention strategy starts with taking three deep breaths. Inhale deeply and then exhale deeply. Just three times. For some, it may help to count as you inhale. 1, 2, 3 to inhale. 1, 2, 3, 4, 5 to exhale. Three times. This will take less than a minute. The simple task of breathing will enhance your awareness and reduce the inordinate attention that was previously fixated on purchasing this object. The simple act of breathing three times starts the process of releasing you from a thought that had previously garnered an inordinate attention. With this perspective change, often your desire reduces and you are in a better position to objectively assess the value of the red shiny object to your life. This simple technique can be performed with eyes open or closed. You can be with your friends at the mall and do this simple breathing exercise without anyone else knowing.

The simple three breath technique is the start of a two-part system. After inhaling and exhaling three breadths, all you have to do is pause for three minutes prior to the impulse buy. This pause and the breath are often sufficient time to neutralize the immediate emotion tied with acquiring a product or service and creates an opening for rational, judicious decision making. The only add-on to this rule is for purchasing a big-ticket item, typically anything over a thousand dollars, where a good night's rest will increase the likelihood that you are buying with a sound, rested mind.

The time intervention techniques slow down your emotions and reduce impulsive decision making. Simply slowing down gives you time to reflect and broadens your attention beyond the tunnel vision. Some people may find meditation helpful in slowing down, others may find spending time in nature to slow down. Slowing down will not come through phones, television and social engagements. It usually comes in solitude. Reading, writing, playing music, and spending quiet time in nature are some of the activities that can help with developing a more contemplative, aware, and self-conscious personality and reduce impulsive behaviors.

## Savings Strategies

Significant savings can be generated from leveraging purchasing strategies. An effective purchasing strategy is conducting competitive bids with three providers. Competitive bidding generates significant uptick in cost reductions, enables selecting reputable vendors and partners, and allows for a better value derivation. Understanding the supply base and the service offerings, a result of conversations with multiple vendors and market scan, allows the buyer to negotiate key terms that reduce costs and help the buyer avoid paying for bells and whistles that do not add value. Introducing competition in the purchasing process typically reduces the cost by 20-30% and can increase value manyfold.

Repeatable purchases such as internet services or cell phone services with monthly service charges or plumbing services wherein a homeowner will likely use such services for their present need and for future needs are good candidates for competitive bids. Competitive bids are also recommended for big-ticket items such as cars, home purchase, and a general contractor for home renovation. The final category wherein competitive bids are highly effective are for services wherein the cost of the service may not be significant but the quality of decision making by the service has an outsized impact on quality of life or cost in another larger category. Architect services and real estate agent services often charge a small percentage of the total project cost, but the quality of their services has major downstream impact on the quality and cost of the deliverable.

Another effective strategy is to buy goods and services when demand is low and retailers are discounting their prices heavily. This phenomenon is common in the retail industry where shelf space is a premium, and the retailers are incentivized to keep products on shelves that have a high turnover, or a high recurring demand.

Effective demand management enables right-sizing the purchasing quantities that match the requirements from an individual or a household. This strategy allows the buyer to buy at lower prices leveraging volume discounts and avoids excessive purchase which will simply clutter up the space, and tie up monies that otherwise could have been invested. Wasteful expenditures are common, and households can save 15-20% by reducing wasteful expenditures. Grocery purchases and pricing plans, whether in a car wash or with internet usage, are examples where matching the purchasing volume with the requirements can deliver savings.

Finally, the buyer must be aware of and be willing to take advantage of the new trends in the market. Technological advancement is driving innovation in every field, and many cost-effective options are popping across industries. An example is the introduction of electric cars, which have reduced car expenditures for operations and maintenance. Another example is the prevalence of streaming companies promoting diverse and accessible media subscriptions and reducing the reliance on an otherwise hefty cable services bill.

The purchasing strategies coupled with application of budgeting, assessment of needs vs wants, and the time intervention techniques to reduce impulse buying increase the savings flowing at the top of the funnel. Leveraging the budget to create a buffer of emergency funds provides a strong backbone to judiciously invest incremental savings and delivers long term growth in wealth. The save to invest strategy reduces the likelihood of available funds spent on unnecessary wants, depleted savings in cash value, and infusing purpose and dynamism by directly linking savings to investing.

# CHAPTER 6

# STRATEGIC DECISION MAKING

A growing body of research shows that willpower used in decision-making is a fixed resource. Though everyone has a different quantity of willpower, the more decisions we make, the more our willpower for decision-making depletes. The subsequent fatigue leads to lower-quality decision-making, especially later in the day. This would explain why many people indulge in cheat foods later in the day even though they had no issues avoiding the same foods earlier in the day.

Simple rich people understand that decision-making depletes willpower and that not all decisions have an equal impact. They try to gain control and influence over strategic decisions crucial to their lives and goals. They also often display a callousness in their involvement with other choices. They are not looking to win and be involved everywhere, just in the places that matter. In that sense, they develop a higher level of judgment, a discerning nature, wherein they first understand what role they would like to play in the decision-making process.

Their discerning nature goes hand-in-hand with wisdom. Often, women will say of simple rich men, "he is so kind," "he listens well," and "he is so attentive." Women feel connected to such men. Women are excellent judges of character, and for any man interested in winning the affections of the opposite sex, these characterizations are essential. As matchmakers will tell you, "It's typically the woman who chooses the man." A simple rich man is kind, listens well, and is attentive. But he is certainly no pushover. He knows when to give in and make others happy (about 95% of the time) and when to exert influence to get his way (about 5%). Because he lets others get their way most of the time, he can stand his ground on what matters to him.

Simple rich people give in on many matters because they are not trying to win everywhere. This behavior may be perceived as a weakness by the uninitiated, but in reality, demonstrates wisdom and strength of character. People who try to win the small battles of life often win alone. Simple rich people try to live with principles and values and are amenable to compromise. They cultivate friendships and relationships which promote symbiotic value. They also are open to the opinions of others, which illuminates their perspective and is a path to learning and growth.

It is profitable in the long run to listen and let others express themselves. Listening to others is the cheapest form of learning. We make decisions constantly, such as what to eat, who is picking up the kids, when to escalate at work, whether to buy or rent, and which car to take to work. Simple rich people ask themselves which decisions matter to their life goals and whether they can automate them. They also develop frameworks to help their decision-making process. These frameworks are only sometimes documented, and they are typically executed automatically. The way to discern these frameworks is to reflect upon their decisions and inquire through inquisitiveness and self-reflection why they were made. There is nothing to hide from yourself, so bare your soul. Honesty is the foundation of this process.

It may help some to document these frameworks, as this may help spot inconsistencies between the framework and your overall goals. For example, suppose a critical life goal is to decrease the consumption of processed food. In that case, a critical decision is whether food is being made at home. Home-made food reduces fast food consumption, which often happens in the evenings after a long day of work. A simple decision could be reserving a specific weekday for outside food as a reward and cooking the remaining days. Cooking at home is often a time saver. A salad bowl can be prepared in a few minutes, as can a healthy bowl of whole wheat pasta, salmon, or rice. It would often take more time to drive to a restaurant. It would also cost more from an outlay of cash in the present, in addition to pinching your wallet long-term by having processed food high in trans fats and sodium.

We often think of time in terms of the immediate day before us and make decisions that seem to save time in the moment. Usually, the relevant industry that benefits, such as the fast-food industry, is influencing our perspective. I encourage you to experiment with an alternative time perspective by taking the long-term view. In doing so, decision-making to save short-term at the expense of the long-term would not seem as rational. For example, if cooking healthy at home most days adds five years to your life, imagine the money you could earn, the time you spend with your loved ones, the places you could travel, and the novel moments you could experience.

Long-term thinking acts as a protective covering against short-changing the quality of our life in the future. This perspective also shields rationality against media influences influencing your decisions in a manner that makes your life convenient in the short term. And so often, even the short-term gains are a fabrication of advertising. According to a 2018 study, ordering from a restaurant is almost five times more expensive than cooking at home. And even a meal kit service is nearly three times as expensive as cooking from scratch.[7] Additionally, cooking a healthy meal with the family is time well spent. Family learns teamwork and relationship building while gaining an apprenticeship in conflict management. Driving to pick up fast food deprives you of family time in the present and cheats you out of your health and those of your loved ones in the long term.

Life satisfaction is linked to the experiences and activities we participate in. Paul Dolan, in his bestselling book *Happiness by Design*, encourages people to focus attention on experiences that promote pleasure and a sense of purpose. A life well lived is often well-lived on an individual's terms. Simple rich people concentrate their time on what matters to them. Some examples are spending time with family, volunteering for a charity, traveling to new places, and learning a new musical instrument. Simple rich people take to heart the adage "time is money." Simple rich people are solving for freedom to manage their time on their terms.

The Time-Money-Value (TMV) framework helps decision activities that align with the judicious use of money and optimize the boon of time. This three-variable framework plots activities with relative impact on time, money, and value to provide a holistic view and force functions thoughtful deliberation to drive decision-making between conflicting priorities.

The foundation of this framework rests on three essential and personal variables—first, the impact of an activity on time. Second, the money being dispensed to achieve that activity. Third, the value the pertinent activity brings to your life. This framework is intended as a guide to help its practitioners, whether nascent or mature, not as an edict. "Time" assesses the impact of an activity concerning how much time it will take. The second variable, "Money," estimates how much money will be required to spend on this activity. The third variable, "Value," estimates the value the action brings to the practitioner's life.

In essence, value forecasts the impact on the quality of life. Value is a judgment call, though not unscientific. Measuring value measures the quality of the experience and the post-experiential outcome. A concert-goer will likely ascribe the value of attending a concert differently than an aspiring musician. It is possible that both rate it as high. However, the concert attendee is measuring it from a lens of experience, while the aspiring musician is measuring it from an additional lens of learning and development. Value puts us in touch with our reality and self-awareness, and the more frequently we use this framework, the better our value estimates get.

Time and money lean quantitative and help assess the feasibility of this activity. As this process is repeated, the practitioners become savvier with their judgments of subjective and objective elements. This framework facilitates decision-making by excluding all other externalities, focusing on three key parameters. It also makes the practitioner accountable and the decision process transparent to the person it matters to the most and whose life it impacts: you.

If someone is interested in learning how to play the piano well, committing fifteen to thirty minutes to daily practice should be sufficient. This amount of time can be taken out of their schedules for most people. The second factor in consideration, money, would vary depending on whether the person plans to hire a private instructor, learn in a class setting with multiple other students, or potentially purchase an app. There are also options for self-learning. There would be additional overlays for purchasing the piano equipment and learning materials.

The intent of understanding the costs of doing an activity is not to discourage progress. On the contrary, considering what it costs prepares the practitioner with complete information. Consideration of cost is an early warning sign for lack of resources. In such case, the course of action may be put it on hold or seek another more creative solution.

Creativity is the cornerstone of the application of intelligence. Creative work is hard work. Creative outcomes lie at the intersection of grit, passion, and drive. Creativity allows human beings to survive and thrive when means are limited. The lack of creativity is often at the root of the turn against good fortune, and often noticed within three generations in opulent families. Unmonitored opulence is usually the cause of stagnation and ruin of individuals and families.

A friend would go to a piano class with his daughter and sit in the piano room with the instructor. While other kids' parents were on their phones checking emails or surfing, he would pay particular attention to the teacher as if he were the student. Not only was he getting a free piano lesson, but it also made him more effective in partnering with his daughter as both grew together in their musical prowess.

Finally, the value component in this example shows the value of music for the individual in question. Value is often the most valuable of the three variables because when one can ascertain the value of an activity to their life, and it comes vis-a-vis the process of self-determination, the individual finds the time and money to do what is of intrinsic value. Writing is a rather laborious process from a time perspective. Still, the value of writing is undeniably significant to the writer, and the growth journey is so palpably felt. Perceived value creates a strong rationale for the investment of time and money.

The TMV framework can be put forth in visual or tabular representations and numerous presentations via the plethora of available technologies can depict a collated view of three variables. My recommendation is a simple one you don't even need a computer for. A napkin will do if you are sitting at a coffee shop and seeking to apply the TMV framework.

In this simple presentation, the impact of each of the other variables is measured below.

Time: Affordable / Stretch / Out of Bounds
Money: Affordable / Stretch / Out of Bounds

Value: Low / Medium / High

| | Affordable | Stretch | Out of Bounds |
|---|---|---|---|
| Time | | | |
| Money | | | |

| | Low | Medium | High |
|---|---|---|---|
| Value | | | |

Out of bounds is a reflection based on the initial or current state for both time and money. Strong desires and creative solutions can move these leftward within stretch and affordability. This assessment puts forth an honest view of what it would take to accomplish a goal and makes compromises self-evident. It also encourages creative problem-solving, and questioning the rules you take for granted and permitting you to liberate yourself from those rules to a world of curiosity, openness, and hope.

We are vessels for harboring miracles, and the TMV framework is a springboard that may help with fast tracking to Station Z. The TMV framework provides a window into the current state and then challenges the practitioner to address the situation by focusing intrinsically and conducting necessary actions to fulfill your most profound dreams and desires. In my experience, I have never needed more time or money to do things I have found to provide excellent value to my life. The time was present, and the money was not a hindrance. The hindrance was always personal habits, and once I looked long and hard at these the time became available, and so did the money.

# CHAPTER 7

# AHOY, CAPTAIN! RUN YOUR LIFE LIKE IT'S YOUR SHIP

People are increasingly plugged into their devices, which are now ubiquitous. The personal computing revolution, which started in the 80s, is changing how people spend time, consume information and communicate with each other. People worldwide have access to mobile devices. Every industry is being reshaped by technology. This change is particularly prominent in the media industry. Consumers have 24/7 access to diverse content delivered by Netflix, Prime, Disney, and many other offerings. One could spend many lifetimes glued to devices, yet we only have one lifetime, one opportunity to connect with ourselves and others in this increasingly virtual world.

The opportunities for impact are boundless, the information has never been so easy to access, and the need is ever so profound. It is often interesting that people who spend a lifetime in their professions advising others fail to heed their words of wisdom. Doctors smoke, financial advisors do not budget, and marriage attorneys cheat.

Simple rich people manage their careers and money with a vision. They leverage technology to further their goals but live in the real world. They inundate themselves with knowledge but question the absurdity of rules and commandments and refuse to follow the herd mindlessly. They understand that work is an essential part of becoming economically self-sufficient and an opportunity for them to spend time developing new skills and building relationships. When simple rich people learn terms such as revenue, income, expenses, budgeting, and debt, they apply these principles to their personal affairs in a manner that mirrors a well-run business.

The learnings from running a business, whether at a small mom-and-pop store or a Fortune 500 company, can be applied directly to one's finances. All households have revenue, expenses, annual budgets, debt, and various categories of costs. Families and individuals can implement annual travel bonus trips to incent achievement of annual savings targets. Households and individuals can implement plans for bringing additional revenue opportunities and design and execute plans to monitor and manage expenses and reduce risk.

Financial terms such as revenues and expenses are managed and reported in small, medium-sized, and large businesses. Applying business terms to personal finances drives rigor and a change of vision and belief. The individual starts thinking of their finances akin to running a ship they commandeer and chart course on. We bring our best to work and apply ourselves to get a paycheck. Wouldn't it be prudent to apply the same principles businesses use to operate and manage to help achieve our financial dreams and aspirations?

Dressing up personal financials in the lion skin of corporate speak is akin to showing up at work in a respectable manner, well-groomed and well-dressed. During the work-from-home days of Covid, there were days I dressed up as if I was going to work. I noticed a difference in how the others communicated with me those days and how it made me feel - alert, confident, and engaged. Ready to rock n roll.

Let's go over some business metrics and translate them for application in the setting of your life. If this feels unnatural, remember that your life is your business. The use of business metrics may seem odd early on, but these will grow on you as you keep up with the formality of the process. A presentation in your job with an appropriate deck dressed in business wear apt for the occasion yields better results than scribbling at the back of a napkin. Running your finances professionally effectively gets you to State Z. Just thinking of your finances in business speak will create an aura of prominence and care for the business of your life. If you approach your finances with focus and respect, levity often will not be far behind and will stay the course. The table below lists the business terminology and its application to manage personal finances.

| Business Metric | Business Metric Definition | Personal Finance Definition |
| --- | --- | --- |
| Revenue | Money generated from normal business operations | Money generated from jobs and / or business ventures plus from investments such as real estate, stocks etc. |
| Expense | Cost that businesses incur in running their operations such as wages, salaries, maintenance, rent etc. | Costs that households incur such as groceries, mortgage, rent, car payments, child care, travel, tax etc. |
| Profit / Loss | Revenue - Expense. If positive, business generates a profit. If negative, it generates a loss. | Revenue - Expense. If positive, household generates a profit. If negative, it generates a loss. |

| Cash Flow | Cash flow refers to the net balance of cash moving into and out of a business.<br><br>Positive cash flow drives higher liquidity. | Cash flow refers to the net balance of cash moving into and out of a household. |
|---|---|---|
| Debt | Amount of money an entity owes. Examples include bank loans, accounts payables and credit card debts | Amount of money that an individual or household owes such as mortgage, car loans, credit card loans etc. |
| Fixed Assets | Long-term assets such as property, plant and equipment that cannot be easily liquidated into cash | Assets such as property, retirement accounts, art, vehicles etc. that cannot be easily liquidated into cash |
| Liquid Assets | Liquid assets allow businesses for fast, easy access to cash. These includes cash on hand, money market funds, stocks etc. | Liquid assets allow individual or households fast, easy access to cash. These would include cash on hand, bank accounts, and stock. |
| Net Worth | Total Assets - Total Liabilities | Total Assets - Total Liabilities |

Businesses use many other financial metrics to measure and optimize their performance. Corporations publish metrics to communicate indicators of financial health and ensure compliance to business stakeholders, including investors, auditors, and regulators. Company management also reviews metrics to manage their business effectively. For individuals and households, the metrics in the table above are sufficient. Though if one wants to go full regalia, I encourage you to share your results and journey. One piece of advice: please do not measure your family by productivity metrics.

This book is focused on the habits of simple rich people and how anyone and everyone can use simple measures to gain transparency into financial health and well-being. Measuring the above metrics with a cadence aptly suits the purpose. Revenue, expenses, and profit/ loss paint a picture of money inflow, outflow, and whether you come out ahead or behind with what you bring in. Focusing on revenue also benefits the way simple rich people approach their jobs. A nine-to-five job is no longer a place to punch in and out; it is a source for revenue generation. This mindset change is life-altering. A source of revenue is a compelling reason to go to work, unlike just a nine-to-five job. When one thinks of a job as an income source, changes happen in what the job means to you and what the job means for you. Individuals get serious about the compensation the job provides and what skills they are developing to continue elevating their value in the marketplace. If channeled positively, individuals may focus on delivering more impact for the organization and have meaningful conversations on how to be appropriately paid for it. It is always a good idea to continuously think about creating a more significant impact for your organization. In a free-market capitalist economy, you can command compensation for your influence. You can switch if your current employer cannot or chooses not to compensate you for the value you bring to the organization.

Alternatively, you can start your own venture to solve a market gap. By doing so, you can become one of the 31 million entrepreneurs in the US and one of the 582 million entrepreneurs worldwide. Changing your lens to focus on a revenue mindset also drives a change in how you view risk from a single source of income. A single source of income is comparable to a business with a single customer. This may incentive some to diversify their risk by adding a side hustle or investments that yield better returns. Thinking of profit/loss and expenses also drive behavioral and mindset changes. Suddenly, even without owning a business, you have the attitude of running your enterprise. John Smith is running John Smith Inc., Alan, and Charlotte Chang are running

Chang Inc, and Marquis Garcia and his son Jose are running Garcia and Son Inc. No business license, additional taxes, bureaucratic paperwork, or financial planning classes. A change that comes intrinsically is a change that permeates and sustains. This is a change that will take you hopping and jumping, and walking, and stumbling, and with added exuberance to Station Z. It's a change that will permeate in time and will reflect a life well lived when you look back at it with pride and ask, "How did I ever do that? I never knew I had it in me..."

Such simple habits, compounded over time, transform simple rich people into the people that the world admires, into women and men that the young generation looks up to, people seek advice from and often wonder whether there was some secret sauce of genetic dispositions or positive forces of circumstances that shaped these lives. For outsiders, these lives could be like palaces that sometimes glitter with gold. But simple rich people often started with their huts long ago when they had just access to straw. Then they built houses of wood. After that, they upgraded to brick houses. Then they built more homes. They were sharpening themselves, often not knowing where they would end up or in the "right" place. With grit and openness to learning, they kept focusing on themselves and simplifying their lives to build the castles of their dreams. Simple rich people are among us. If you are a simple rich person, please take a bow and guide the rest. And if you aren't, apply yourself and have faith in yourself. You will build your castles. It will take time, but you will have no fear once you build them. It is better to be a mason who knows how to build a castle than a king who inherits it.

The mason knows how to build a castle, where the frailties are and when and where to apply reinforcements. When applied to our personal lives, these eight-business metrics provide us guidance and visibility to improve the management of our personal finances. We covered the first three metrics earlier in this chapter; the remaining five are covered next.

Cash flow is the amount of money that flows in and out. It is a material indicator of your financial health and a leading indicator of what is yet to come. It prepares the mason to reflect on upcoming potential pitfalls and add reinforcements to mitigate future risks. Debt is the amount of money owed by individuals or households. Debt is correlated with your physical health, and a palatable debt is a must for Station Z. Fixed and liquid assets comprise your assets, with liquid assets reflecting easily accessible assets that can help with meeting obligations and surfing with the twists and turns of waves in life.

Liquid assets are troops at your disposal that you can count on for immediate relief. Your liquid assets should cover your emergency funds available in cash and bank accounts for six to twelve months, depending on whether you are single or have childcare or adult care responsibilities. Stocks are also liquid assets but should not be counted toward emergency funds. Given the fluctuations in the stock market, the goal is to sell stocks at an opportune time to make a profit or cut losses if the stock is not performing well. If you are following the investing strategy of Mr. Warren Buffett, arguably the world's greatest investor, the goal is to hold stocks for an extended period. I follow Mr. Buffett's advice and am a long-term shareholder in Mr. Buffett's investment conglomerate Berkshire Hathaway. Though stocks are liquid, these should not count toward emergency funds. This strategy incentivizes long-term thinking when investing in stocks.

Nothing like cash gives one peace of mind to deal with life's emergencies. Even though cash is a poor investment in the long term due to inevitable inflation, it is like having a village doctor who lives at home, will attend to your needs at odd hours, and will give you the sage advice we all need in times of distress. "Eat well, don't take too much stress, be optimistic, and most importantly it's all going to be ok." The village doctor may not possess the financial wherewithal of the surgeons or doctors in big cities. The village doctor may not present at conferences or awarded medals like political appointees do. However, the village doctor practices medicine with the sensitivity of someone who knows the patient and their history. Your cash is your village doctor. Unassuming, kind, and available, should you choose to honor it. It may not be something you boast about regarding investment returns, but its presence gives you the confidence and courage to deploy your other assets.

Net worth is an objective indicator of your wealth. Many people weigh themselves frequently and have a reasonable sense of how much their weight is. However, a tiny minority have precise knowledge of their weight. Many people may claim they are wealthy, but facts are more substantive than mere presentment. Having precise knowledge of one's wealth is vital. Of all the metrics discussed, this is the starting metric. The weight indicated on the weighing machine is not a comprehensive indicator of your health but is a good starting point. Similarly, net worth is a starting point, and those who know their net worth have the magic carpet to get to State Z. I would highly encourage you to calculate your net worth with a monthly frequency to the uninitiated, and once the habit sets in, you can switch to quarterly. Apple has quarterly results, Amazon has it, eBay has it, Google has it, GE has it, and so should you. And you can start today. Stop reading. Start your computer and download the net worth template provided on simplerichpeople.com. Once you are in a steady state, it will take you no more than fifteen minutes to calculate.

An apt analogy for the metrics to manage personal finances is sports. Some metrics form your defensive line, others as your offensive line, and a third category can serve as both. Debt is a defensive back for football fans. In life as in sports, the stronger your defense, the more freedom your offense has to push for gains. The confidence to go on the offense emanates from the ability to withstand losses. Debt, being our obligations, is the titular metric that has a bearing on our offensive strategy. This is why many financial health gurus, such as Dave Ramsey, advocate paying off mortgages and keeping debt low.

Expenses is another defensive back. Expenses managed transparently and strategically becomes a solid defensive back that defines your ability to take risk and withstand setbacks. Liquid assets, profit/loss, and cash flow are metrics that initially play a defensive role but if deployed effectively can play on the offense and start scoring touchdowns over time. Revenue is an offensive metric. Fixed assets, typically comprising real estate and retirement accounts, are also offensive metrics. Savvy investors invest in fixed assets with discretionary funds, prioritizing this to ensure long-term wealth. Your net worth is neither offensive nor defensive. It defines your position on the playing field. The role of the offensive and defensive metrics is to keep furthering you toward your goals because, in the State of Z, you are playing for your empowered life. You are playing for your freedom and living a fulfilling and financially worry-free life.

There is immense value in thinking about and verbalizing these metrics as part of your discourse within your family and to yourself. As any athlete or musician knows, change happens with repetition. Once the repetition is set in its way, the amount of willpower it takes to repeat the behavior reduces significantly. The benefits of automated behaviors were covered earlier. As the person starts using these terms in managing their finances, the care and decision-making around personal finances becomes structured and meticulous and involve thoughtful considerations. These eight metrics should be considered and, where applicable, reflected in the TMV framework discussed previously. These would be typically covered in the Money parameter of the TMV framework discussed in the previous chapter, though they may also find a home in Time and Value sporadically.

Using these terminologies also impacts how important your money feels to you. Money is a channel for achieving our dreams and enabling a life of our choice. Any medium pivotal to living a life of fulfillment and impacting our well-being should merit serious consideration and be one of our highest priorities. Every individual's life is as important as what the individual believes to be. This is not intended to vote for hedonism or conceited behavior but for self-care and self-belief. It also advances the cause of human dignity and kindness, as those who are comfortable with themselves develop a greater degree of empathy for others.

Another benefit to formalizing the life of your finances with the cloak of the business world is that it fundamentally changes your relationship with money. Ah, yes, you read it right. You are in a relationship with money. For many people, far too many, the relationship with money is one-sided. In this relationship, we use the money to get what we want and dispose of it. However, there is a higher spiritual relationship with money where money stops being a tool to get what we want and, instead, a partner to enjoy our life and liberties.

When money is just an object of use, it satisfies our immediate needs. A positive symbiotic relationship occurs when money starts shifting to become a resource we care for and a medium to grow us personally and professionally. Money helps us grow, and money grows for us. And oddly enough, our craving for money diminishes, and our attachment to the dollars and cents lessens because now we are in a positive relationship with money. A positive relationship is built on our elevated sense of maturity with how we view money not anymore as a tool to get more stuff but as a resource to learn from and grow with.

The true riches at Station Z are not reflected by "how much do you have" but by "how well do you live." "How much" is defined by our material possessions. It makes most people feel inadequate. How well one lives is a reflection of the thoughts and feelings inside. Blind pursuit of money will only add misery to one's life. Leveraging money to build a life of your dreams is a surefire ticket to happiness. In the process, effectively managing finances becomes so ingrained that it is effortless. Like a musician becoming one with the music, a dancer becoming one with the performance, and a programmer becoming one with coding, managing money flows. We don't judge ourselves or others based on material possessions. It reflects a relationship of acceptance and peace. An association of sufficiency, not portrayal. A relationship of benevolent gratitude at mastering one of the most challenging human proclivities: conquering the wild rush for more possessions and the never-ending anxiety in that journey.

CHAPTER 8

# BUDGETING

"You can't manage what you can't measure." Edward Deming was an American engineer, statistician, and management consultant. He is considered the father of the quality revolution. Deming consulted and influenced Toyota and Sony to improve product quality. Deming believed that if you cannot measure something, you cannot manage it because your judgments and decisions are not based on facts. A budget is designed to create a fact-based baseline for expenditures.

Budgeting is a process of planning for your financial expenditures. It is a thoughtful, deliberate process that puts your spending front and center. If done objectively and honestly, there is no place to hide from the truth of our spending. The process is not intended to be a shaming but a learning process. It can be a fun and engaging process, similar to playing an exploratory video game where one learns the landscape of a new universe—the gamer and protagonist further her skills to survive and thrive in this new environment.

Budgeting powers our self-awareness and self-reflection. Budgeting helps us acknowledge who we are and where we are financially. It allows us to go on a journey to State Z. When most of us go on vacations, especially with kids, we spend the night before or the morning packing. We pack our clothes, toiletries, and documentation such as passports and pack for activities we plan on going. Maybe scuba gear or bicycle shorts. Sunscreens and medicines. Parents with children, especially younger ones, have many more things to prepare for. Baby food, diapers, baby wipes, the list could go on. The planning helps us stay on course for this new travel adventure. Uncertainties on the trip may arise, but we feel better equipped if we have our toolbox with us. Budgeting is much like preparing for going on a trip. It is a plan for how much we spend in a specific timeframe, often a calendar year, and then monitoring it to see how we perform against that plan.

Budgeting is a prerequisite to running a business. Any company big or small budgets. How well the budgeting process goes is often an indicator correlated with the company's financial well-being and culture. Do managers take budgeting seriously? Or is it just a check-the-box exercise? Once budgets are set, is there monitoring of how the plans perform against expectations? Are managers held accountable for meeting / performing better against the budget target? Is there a financial incentive or penalty for the managers to meet the target?

In the last chapter, I made a cogent (I hope) case for people to run their finances like a business, the business of life. That argument is extended to the budget. The good news is that personal budgets are nowhere as complicated as corporate budgets, where often the complications are political and related to data accessibility. And with many different tools in the market, maintaining a budget is straightforward. This chapter will cover the budgeting process to prepare you for creating one. A sample budgeting template is available in downloadable format at simplerichpeople.com. Though you may use many available apps, I highly recommend conducting a budget the old-fashioned way of manually categorizing the expenses for at least the first year. Seeing your expenses first-hand gives you a better lay of the land, just like driving around a new city will provide you with a better sense of the roads than depending on GPS.

Let's take a simple example of a budget. Brian makes $300 monthly from his part-time job at the mall. He also gets a $100 allowance from his parents for a monthly income of $400. He is responsible for the running expenditure for his car, excluding car insurance and car loan payments, which are taken care of by his parents. He is also responsible for his travel, leisure, and hobbies.

Though his monthly income is fixed, his expenses have fixed and variable components. Eating patterns, gas prices, and car usage drive variability, and he estimates based on historical averages. The cost of guitar classes and club membership is fixed. Brian pays a monthly fee of $50 for guitar lessons and a club membership of $60. He estimates $90 for eating and $50 for gas. Coming from a family that owns a small business, Brian knows the value of savings for emergencies and saves 10% to his emergency savings fund, leaving him with $110. He estimates another $60 monthly for entertainment activities with friends, such as concert tickets. Brian has a few choices for the $50 remainder. He can contribute to his savings or spend additional money on things he prefers to buy or experience. He can also work less if he needs more study time or other activities. His choice is driven by actual data reflecting his current financial situation. A thorough awareness of his financial situation prevents decision-making with a tunnel view. So what does Brian do? Brian donates $10 to his local animal shelter monthly and the remaining $40 to his savings. Of his $400 income, he contributes 10% to his emergency fund and another 10% to his savings for $80 per month. He is also contributing to his cause of helping animals, and he can budget for his hobbies, sports, and leisure activities. Had lucid data not been available, Brian's ability to make effective decisions would have been constrained.

Let's explore a slightly more complicated example of a typical American household. Sara and Matt are married with a three-year-old son, Jonathan. Both are working full-time at a high-tech company. Their jobs bring $180,000 and post-tax household income of $120,000, or

$10,000 monthly. Sara and Matt did not keep a budget until recently when they got behind on their credit card payments and an uncle, a financial advisor by profession, advised them to do so.

Keeping a budget for a couple of months now, Sara and Matt gained valuable insights into their spending categories, listed below in Table SM (sorted in descending order of expenditure amount).

| Spending Category | Amount |
|---|---|
| Mortgage | $2,000 |
| Child Care | $1,500 |
| Car Payment 1 | $1,500 |
| Travel | $1,250 |
| Eating Out | $1,000 |
| Grocery | $750 |
| Car Payment 2 | $500 |
| Gas | $500 |
| Utilities | $500 |
| Home Related Purchases | $500 |
| Miscellaneous Purchases | $500 |
| Cleaning Services / Gardening Services | $300 |
| Car Insurance / Home Insurance | $200 |
| Total | $11,000 |

Table SM

A simple two-month exercise delivered many a-ha and duh! moments. To their credit, Sara and Matt faced the stone-cold facts with courage. Not doing so will only increase debt-induced stress for first-time parents. Taking no action as a strategy will only exacerbate their financial issues. Given their responsibility to provide for Jonathan's well-being and educational expenses, having no emergency fund, no college fund, and no savings opens them to risks and much stress, especially if one or both lose their jobs. Revenue is only one side of the personal finance equation; expenses are equally important. Considering they make forty times more than Brian and are in a significantly riskier position is a testament to the importance of budgeting and expense management.

Armed with data, Sara and Matt have several options, varying in impact and effort. Given their $1,000 shortfall, a car payment of $1,500 is a drag on their expenses. They can immediately sell their car and buy a value-for-money used car. Another opportunity for improvement is travel at $1,250 and eating out at $1,000. These discretionary expenditures are $2,250 monthly, more than 20% of the household's post-tax income. If they adjust to budget vacations, reduce eating out by 40% (this will reflect an increased grocery bill), and value for money car, a $1,500 savings could be realized toward an emergency fund. The result is a significantly better outcome than their current state of running behind $1,000. With just two months of budgeting and an attitude that reflected fact-based problem-solving and dexterity of approach, Sara and Matt are on their way to the State of Z.

Budgeting is a straightforward process of planning expenses by spend categories and tracking the plan's progress. This allows for a fact-based understanding of spending patterns. Delicately simple. Remarkably effective. High implementation rates?

Most households do not budget. According to a Gallup poll, only 32% of American households have a budget.[8] These households are also correlated with having a long-term financial and savings plan. This is not entirely unexpected, like the doctors who smoke, the tax attorneys who lie on their taxes, or the financial advisors who do not diversify their investments. Solutions are always more straightforward on paper. Our fast-paced lives, fears, and emotions make implementing simple, groundbreaking plans harder.

The reasons why people don't budget are not complicated. There are common misconceptions about the process that inhibit many people from starting or persisting with it. A common reason for not budgeting is an arcane fear of math. Numbers tend to make people uncomfortable. But this is not calculus, linear algebra, or any version of advanced math. No math degree is required for budgeting. It's simple addition and subtraction. Budgeting is not complex math; it is a representation of the spending habits of your life. A way to understand, manage and improve their lives. A medium for people to better understand themselves. Spreadsheets like Excel and Google Sheets eliminate any need for manual calculations and allow you to automate and systemize the process.

Another reason is lower prioritization of finances ahead of all other busy work. The solution here is simple. Budgeting is essential to manage your finances effectively. There are many paths to happiness, but it is only possible with satisfaction with your financial health. It is often, and unfortunate, when even wealthy people do not find happiness and contentment that the actual value of money offers as the nectar of life. Budgeting fosters contentment and feeling grounded because having a great deal of money is not the same as knowing you have enough. If you gain only one habit from this book, it is budgeting. The process is rewarding. Be honest. Be ethical. Do not aim for perfection. Give it your best.

The third reason for not budgeting is the pervasive overconfidence bias. Overconfidence bias reflects a feeling, or at worst, an ideology that reflects confidence without the absence of knowledge. Overconfidence often hides a genuine discomfort to face the truth. At its foundation, the budgeting process reflects the financial picture as it is and not as we wish. Knowledge and self-effacing humility are adequate antidotes to ignorance. Your current financial situation is a reflection of your circumstances and your habits till this moment. It is not a medium to drive guilt. It is a channel to drive growth. Budgeting is a framework for building a brighter future. Budgeting can be an engaging and self-revealing journey best undertaken with curiosity and openness.

The fourth common reason is letting the fear of failure or wanting to be perfect create an image of budgeting as a process only for the gifted. Most human worries are irrational, and fears around numbers or discipline should be stared down till you see the puppy and no longer the lion. Budgeting, like any process, is a skill the preparer will improve on and customize over time. This invitation for creativity should instead spur the naysayers into action.

Budgeters do not have particular degrees, special skills, or special training. They are not all gifted. They are not all eloquent. They are not all college graduates. They are not all wealthy. They are not all CEOs. Many talented, articulate, wealthy college graduates do not budget. Like any new skill, budgeting can be learned. It is one of the most valuable and practical life skills to learn. This is not calculus, whose use, you may wonder. This is the class that schools should offer in addition to calculus. Here are a few findings from Dave Ramsey's *The State of Personal Finance in America 2022*.

- Only 45% of Americans said they have at least $1,000 in savings, and over a third (36%) have no savings.
- One in five Americans have fallen deeper into debt since June of 2022, and only 24% said they reduced their debt.
- In the last quarter, half of Americans said their finances adversely impacted their mental health.
- Younger generations are more worried about their finances than older generations (71% of Gen Z compared to 42% of baby boomers) - showing an inverse correlation between worry and experience.

The following section will walk you through creating a budget. A template for budgeting can be downloaded from simplerichpeople. com.

## Creating a Budget

Creating a budget involves first preparing a target for savings and expense categories, and then tracking actual expenses against it. The comparison tracks actual performance on savings goals and expenditures. It's not a complicated process. It's a fact-based, data-driven process to give you a picture of your finances, which helps you manage them. If the truth sounds mundane, think of yourself as a pirate on a treasure hunt. Aye, aye, matey, get that metal detector, and let's do some treasure hunting! And absolutely no pillaging of another's property. This is all going to be sacrosanct and limited to our journey. No more time to dilly-dally. Ahrrr!

## Budgeting Process

The budgeting process starts with creating expense categories and defining what those categories entail. The expense categories should be simple enough to avoid confusion (yes, it happens to everyone and will happen to you!), and try to have at most ten to fifteen categories. Less than ten is okay as well. Expense categories should align with spending patterns. As the budgeting process matures, analytics are leveraged to understand, influence and shape behaviors. Grouping categories that are closely linked together is a recommended approach. For example, travel, eating out, and activities such as concerts may be merged under a single category, such as leisure. This is not a rule but a recommendation that may work for some people. For others, having travel as a separate category may make greater sense if the granular visibility of travel expenses is desirable. I encourage you to bring your individuality with gusto and passion in this process. You will then own it, and it will grow on you.

Spend categories change as your life progresses—life events such as marriage and having kids change spending habits and add new expenditures. There may be existing categories that have a drop in spending. As you get closer to understanding your spending, categories will also change, as will sometimes the scope of a category. Though I will share common categories, and you can certainly leverage these, I encourage you to tweak. Be creative. Be colorful. Be vibrant. This is your painting. I am just starting you off with helpful supplies. Common spending categories are mortgage, home repair, grocery, personal care, travel, eating out, child care, pet care, medical, fitness, tax, gas, car payment, utilities, insurance, gifts, education, charity, etc.

Once the categories are defined (Step 1), you allocate the anticipated spending for each type. For first-timers, I recommend going through at least the last three months of your past expenditures on all your credit cards and bank statements to assess your expenditures. A six-month picture would provide a better view of your expenses as non-recurring expenses get better reflected with a longer time frame. And of course, if you want an A+, do the exercise for the last year. Explore your expense statements by putting on music or a movie you watched before. Don't judge yourself by your expenditures, observe.

There are three benefits of going through your expenditures and categorizing them in your first draft categories. The first is getting a fact-based picture of spending habits. It is likely (almost certain) that you will be surprised and say Aha! a few times. "I didn't realize I spent so much on eating out." "Wow, my car payments are a big portion of my spending." This may often be followed by a self-directed Socratic process, a rather quaint and spiritual experience. "Hmm, why are my car related expenses so high?" Or, "The grocery bill seems small compared to our bills for eating out." The questions often lead to more questions, in a spiraling waterfall leading you to observe your habits. The harmless inquiry about grocery bills could stumble you to a path of investigating eating habits of where and how often you eat. Don't be surprised if you connect the dots with spending habits and the derived satisfaction and value. "Wow, I spend $2,000 on gym membership, and I don't go. Why is that? Well, I don't like crowded indoor spaces. I much prefer hiking." Spirituality is in progress.

I enjoy socializing with friends. Through self-inquiry, I recognize that it is the time we spend, not the food. This led to a change in habits to activity-based social settings such as hiking with friends instead of eating and drinking in restaurants or pubs. Habits have the power to change who we socialize with and can garner appreciation from many others influenced by our ability and willingness to change. Hikers often befriend other hikers, just as bikers befriend other bikers.

The second benefit of going through the expenditure review process is that the margin of error with forecasting for spend categories reduces. Many expenditures, such as groceries, have recurring patterns—a previous year's baseline with an inflation escalator can provide a reasonably accurate budget target for the next cycle. Barring a life event like having a child, grocery spending patterns are unlikely to change. If one is looking to increase intake of organic food, this also serves as an opportunity to tweak based on the habits you envisage setting and the changes you expect in life.

The third benefit is improved spend categorization. Spend categories will change as you learn more about your expenditures. Understanding the landscape of your expenses gives you a massive leap of knowledge and trust in the process and allows you to generate pertinent categories. Pivoting to categories that reflect your life priorities will enable you to digest information and make actionable decisions. It's a continuous journey, with frequent tweaking in the earlier stages of the process.

Let's take the example of Kate. Kate's goals are to have a balanced budget and to save for a 10% emergency fund. She refers to this pouch of money as the "umbrella fund." Kate's expenses are listed in the table below.

| Spend Category | Monthly Spend |
|---|---|
| Rent | $1,000 |
| Tax | $1,000 |
| Clothes / Accessories | $500 |
| Car Payment 1 | $500 |
| Travel | $350 |
| Student Loans | $300 |
| Grocery | $300 |
| Eating Out | $250 |
| Utilities | $100 |
| Miscellaneous Purchases | $100 |
| Gas | $50 |
| Medical Insurance | $50 |
| Total | $4,500 |

Table Kate-I

In a balanced budget, expenses do not exceed income; Kate's pre-tax monthly income is $5k, and her post-tax income is $4k. It is the pre-tax income that expenses must be measured against because taxes are also an expenditure. Her expenses add to $4,500. So, she has a balanced budget because her expenses do not exceed her income. In addition, she is saving $500, which meets the 10% emergency fund target.

But the story of life is ever-winding. Cupid strikes Kate during a visit to the animal shelter, and she walks out with Mara, a Labrador retriever. Along with gaining a new friend, Kate also gains more expenses. Dog care costs are $350 a month, and Kate starts contributing $100 to the Humane Society to advocate for better treatment of animals. As the table below illustrates, total expenses are $4,950. Kate still has a balanced budget but can no longer save sufficiently for an emergency umbrella fund.

| Spend Category | Monthly Spend |
|---|---|
| Rent | $1,000 |
| Taxes | $1,000 |
| Clothes / Accessories | $500 |
| Car Payment 1 | $500 |
| Travel | $350 |
| Student Loans | $300 |
| Grocery | $300 |
| Dog Care | $350 |
| Eating Out | $250 |
| Utilities | $100 |
| Miscellaneous Purchases | $100 |
| Humane Society | $100 |
| Gas | $50 |
| Medical Insurance | $50 |
| Total | $4,950 |

Table Kate-II

In her monthly tracking, Kate realizes she needs to meet her financial goals and cuts back on eating out, travel, and clothes and accessories to meet both objectives. Kate's example exemplifies the power of budgeting, as she uses knowledge of her expenses to shift her behaviors that bring positivity, love, and vibrance to her life. This is the power of money working for Kate!

| Spend Category | Monthly Spend |
|---|---|
| Rent | $1,000 |
| Taxes | $1,000 |
| Clothes / Accessories | $250 |
| Car Payment 1 | $500 |
| Travel | $250 |
| Student Loans | $300 |

| | |
|---|---|
| Grocery | $300 |
| Dog Care | $350 |
| Eating Out | $150 |
| Utilities | $100 |
| Miscellaneous Purchases | $100 |
| Humane Society | $100 |
| Gas | $50 |
| Medical Insurance | $50 |
| Total | $4,500 |

Table Kate-III

## Starting Your Budget

The habit of budgeting will deliver the most bang for your buck. You can download a budget template from simplerichpeople.com, or create your own using popular spreadsheet programs such as Excel, Google Sheets, or Numbers for Apple users. Tracking budgets has become considerably more straightforward with online access. For cash payments, you still need to itemize your receipts for budget tracking for placement in the appropriate spending categories. In the initial stages of habit forming, when it feels challenging or cumbersome, equip yourself with the knowledge that budgeting is not tricky, but change is. The hardness factor significantly reduces as you repeat the process, and many people report enjoying tinkering with their spending habits. It is like playing a video game where you are the designer and the protagonist. Improving our habits becomes part of our core, and we should feel proud of it, knowing that our practices are creating a better life for us and a sense of empowerment. A feeling that we are driving our car, not just a passenger reacting to circumstances around us.

Tracking expenses may initially seem daunting to the uninitiated. There are several ways to track spending, and I will share a few of these. Which one you choose depends on many factors, primarily influenced by the mediums you choose for payments. The payments ecosystem has expanded significantly with PayPal, credit cards, debit cards, Venmo, Zelle, and cash, still the handsome hunk next door. Successful expense tracking is a function of consistently keeping up with the process and strategically leveraging payment channels to simplify the recording process. Repetition and consistency drive the formation of habits. The more straightforward the process, the easier to repeat, and the higher the chances of successful habit forming.

One way to track your expenses is the cash-envelope system. Essentially, this means you have a cash envelope for each spending category, and when you spend money, you take money from that envelope and make a note on your phone or notebook. The phone is always more accessible; pieces of paper can get lost, make up for an obese wallet, and may even add a few pounds to your butt. I always prefer digital for ease of transfer via email. Digital copies facilitate the analysis of spending habits and serve as a blueprint for your progress.

Digital copies bring the power of BIG DATA to your spending habits. Digital records allow for analytics. You do not need to be a math whiz to harness the power of data. Insights and willingness to act upon them often correlate with curiosity and openness. Being comfortable with challenging our worldview and accepting reality even when it presents a seemingly contradictory view to our belief systems opens the door for meaningful insights.

The simplicity of the insight often results from sustained problem-solving. In other words, stay in the game. When Charles Darwin theorized evolution, the simplicity of the theory left him astounded. When Sherlock Holmes finds the solution, the simplicity of his thinking process leads him to what he later describes as self-evident. However, even though something is simple, it takes work. This universal life principle applies leaps and bounds to managing personal finances. Personal finance is not the divine domain of financial experts and Mensa members. You do not need a prestigious degree from a top-notch school. It is simply a function of your habits. Your simplicity is your strength, your character is your armor, and your humility is a blessing. Anyone can leverage basic analytics with consistency to drive extraordinary results.

I recommend the digital method of recording expenses over the cash-envelope method. Digital payments include credit cards, debit cards, e-check and mobile wallets. However, there is a significant benefit to using cash over digital payments where possible. Paying via credit cards drives more spending than purchasing with hard cash. A study conducted by Dunn & Bradstreet found that people spend 12-18% more when using credit cards. McDonald's reports its average purchase is $7 when people use credit cards versus $4.50 for cash - an increase of 55%![9] However, there are disadvantages to using the cash envelope system. First, carrying cash in different envelopes is cumbersome and can be annoying. It can also put you at a more considerable loss if you are a theft target. And then there are the social aspects. Imagine going out with your friends for a movie and trying to ascertain which envelope to take the money from. You could rush to a restroom to access the cash envelope system, which would lead to frequent restroom trips, and your friends may be left with an impression of your digestive tract needing a visit from the plumber.

The second method for expense tracking involves a monthly walkthrough and categorizing transactions from credit cards, banks, and digital wallets such as Venmo. Transactions on cards are easy to access and manage. In this method, any payments by cash must be recorded manually. I use this method to get credit card rewards like points, cash back, etc., except at a gas station where cash yields lower pricing. When adopting this strategy, select a card with rewards points, cash back, etc., and make timely payments. You still have to track and stick to a budget, so if you are spending a lot more simply because of the ease of the credit card, rein in your spending or switch to the cash envelope system. With credit cards, extra vigilance must be maintained to avoid spending money because of the smooth, frictionless experience of the card. You are still accountable for the money you spend on the card - it is a loan from the bank that comes at a very high-interest rate.

Using a debit card is a middle-of-the-road approach allowing for a convenient payment experience with systemic controls. Avoid signing up for the overdraft service with debit cards to limit your spending. Debit cards limit spending to your available balance and create more checks and balances than credit card purchases. As you feel more comfortable with your spending habits and financial situation, you may use credit cards to get rewards. The suggestions in this book are guidelines for you to experiment with and create a system of habits that works for you. These are yours to develop and learn more about yourself. Feel free to experiment with your budgeting process and spending habits. If nothing else, it will add a bit of spice to your life. And you will have a story to tell.

At a party recently, I was chatting with a charismatic and intelligent woman. She worked in a large technology company and is a mother of three kids. We were discussing financial empowerment, and I inquired if she budgets. She said no. But what she said after was intriguing. She said she would be "uncomfortable to find out how much and where I spend." She was so refreshingly honest about herself, and I couldn't imagine this tiger mom cowered by the truth.

The tiger mom's comment is not an uncommon reason why budgeting is avoided. The argument is similar to claims that checking one's weight would cause distress or that going for regular checkups with the doctor may lead to information that we would instead feel comfortable without. In all such cases, aren't we already in discomfort? The discomfort of the unwillingness to face the facts continues to nag at us, and effort needs to be dispensed to distract us from simple realities. There is more significant discomfort in not being honest with ourselves about the facts and proclivities that shape us who we are. Honesty with ourselves is the best policy because it is the most effective means to drive meaningful change. Self-acceptance and embracing the present circumstances pave the way for a calmer and self-reliant self. Managing personal finances is a journey of self-awareness. It is not intended to be a competition against others or another condescending judgment criterion for how we are falling short. It is an opportunity to learn and grow.

# CHAPTER 9

# SPEND CATEGORIES: THE ART & SCIENCE OF BUDGETING

Budget is an evolving painting of your finances; spend categories are the color palettes you, the artist, use to draw the masterpiece. Spend categorization provides visibility to the products and services we spend our money on. Expenses are bucketed into various spend categories driving spend transparency, facilitating informed changes to spending habits, and measuring progress against desired change.

Though there are some common spending areas, and I will suggest a few that you could use, your categories are unique to your worldview. You can order this burger animal style, a 4x4 patty, or without any buns. This is your painting, Picasso. Use the colors that flow for you and keep at your work of art. And as your life changes, the categories will change accordingly. Categories reflect your present life and the life you want to build. Spend categories are tools supporting changing priorities. They reflect who you are today and who you want to transform into.

The categories are static in time yet fluid in the long run of your journey. Going to college, getting married, getting a job, having kids, changing careers, and supporting aging parents will influence spending habits.

People in similar life stages will have different categories, reflecting their personalities and preferences. Changing priorities in life at any stage leads to changes in spending patterns. This is where creating a budget and tracking expenditures has an outsized impact on achieving life goals beyond financials. It paints a picture of your habits, which must be changed to accomplish personal goals and drive change. This change process is internal to you, me, and everyone else. Change always comes from within.

Some typical categories are grocery, house items, mortgage, rent, child care, utilities, gas, grooming, tuition, travel, entertainment, and miscellaneous, which is an ensemble of unrelated items. These categories are common, and I encourage you to add new categories to suit your life priorities. Nomenclature is also up to you. Miscellaneous can be renamed as "a bunch of unrelated crap." The only guideline for categories is clearly defining them and avoiding the proliferation of categories to drive meaningful insights. Ten to fifteen categories would be a good balance for most, though less than ten could also be conducive.

Though size matters with spending to qualify a spend as meaningful, categories with low spend can also provide meaningful insights and be focus areas. An example would be to focus on types where a focused reduction or increase in spending is a priority. For example, Jane, a smoker since college and an executive in her early forties, is thinking of conceiving. She has a huge incentive to quit smoking. Jane adds smoking as a category (previously part of the Miscellaneous category). Jane's monthly expense is a paltry $100 compared to mortgage, car payment, travel, eating out, entertainment shows, grocery, gas, charity, and home renovations. But by adding this category, Jane explicitly monitors smoking expenditures to reduce and eliminate her habit.

Similarly, Ji-Hyun is a corporate attorney in her early forties. A life with long working hours and two kids takes a toll. It's been dawning on

Ji-Hyun that she needs to focus on her fitness and mental well-being to improve the quality and longevity of her life. Ji-Hyun tweaks her budget to create two categories: Kickass Attorney (for personal fitness) and Monk's in Town (for mental well-being). Attorneys can have fun too! The Kickass Attorney category includes gym membership, chiropractor services, and acupuncture services. These are activities she is currently enrolled in. Monk's In Town covers therapy sessions and spa services. In addition, Ji-Hyun also adds activities such as horse riding and salsa classes to enhance her mental well-being. Ji-Hyun's categorization indicates the flexibility one can apply to the budgeting framework. And because you can customize the framework to fit your life's needs, it is yours to keep, follow, and tweak.

Selecting categories and tracking expenses is scientific because it is rooted in quantitative data to provide an objective reality that the language of numbers provides. It also allows the budgeter to be creative and personalize this process. Use the science of budgeting while spraying with the graffiti of your unique personality and perspectives.

The power of personal finances and feeling wealthy is not derived from static truisms. These powers come from experimenting and developing habits. Simple rich people struggle like everyone else and fail more than others. Creating new ways of working requires constant experimentation. A willingness to evaluate, accept and tweak is at the heart of successful experimentation. This process also leads to significant growth and pushes the boundaries of what we deem possible and realistic. It also makes life's journey enjoyable because it adds a dash of unpredictability to it. Simple rich people lead extraordinary lives. Sometimes, these lives may be reflected in the media. However, most such lives are limited to the awareness of close friends and relatives. The courage to experiment leads to a radiance that inspires others around them and is a channel to fuel their curiosities and lead a self-determined fascinating life.

Simple decisions such as leading a healthy life can carry an allure of an intricate maze. It is the many possibilities of navigating the maze that a simple rich person finds irresistible and deeply engaging. A person pursuing a healthy life can make inroads via several routes. Eating less processed food, avoiding fast food, making food at home, purchasing organic fruits and vegetables, improving mental health by meditation or taking coaching classes, and improving fitness by playing sports are a fraction of the possibilities. Add to these potential changes in grocery purchasing habits, eating habits, socializing, frequency of bar visits, and whether one chooses water or soda while eating out. The possibilities are boundless. Even changes of basic levels in one or more of these habits drive long-term benefits as an outcome and to the protagonist willing to go on a transformative journey. As one grows accustomed to change, changing habits becomes a lifestyle. We form habits continuously; what is positively different is the expansion and rate of conscious habit formation.

If any of this is overwhelming, think of your life as a maze, your habits as your allies in this game, and a reflection of your current skill set and personal growth as the resulting outcome. You are the mouse trying to get to the cheese. You will need to pursue different and traverse difficult paths. There will be paths that will end up as dead-ends. Then you will change course and try alternatives. Sometimes, you may need to return to the starting position and reevaluate your strategy. Why? Because you want the cheese. Sure, you can tell yourself that you don't want the cheese. But you know deep within your heart that it's not the cheese you crave. It is just a ruse to encourage you to engage, explore and connect.

We were not born to be static phantoms ogling our phones. We were born to explore, connect, move, dance, listen, learn, teach, and grow. Habits are a euphemism for how to traverse the maze of life. As young kids, we love to do mazes. Yet, when we grow older, many of us want the next generation to do mazes but somehow give ourselves a reprieve for engaging in the game of life. The game of life is a game of habits. Our habits are our assets and liabilities. At a basic level, we have a dichotomous choice.

Either we accept that we can change and take the challenge of the maze of life or sit in front of a television or phone, give up on our potential, and drown ourselves in the noises around us. The feeling of a better alternative will haunt us. And it will nag at us. We can numb that noise with smoking, media, drugs, and alcohol, but we know in our solitary moments the beautiful gift that we are squandering. People are often afraid of death, yet every day we give in to the numbness; we are dying slowly. This choice decision governs how we approach our health, education, relationships, energy levels, and finances. Budgeting is the mechanism to make that choice for improving your habits to manage personal finances.

The journey of our habits is unique to our personalities, perspectives, and circumstances. It's her story and history. It's they-story and them-story. A simple and seemingly uninteresting grocery category can illustrate individuality and liberation. Hmm, rather dull, you say. Keep on reading.

Rosie has a family of three, including her husband and their eight-year-old daughter. They mainly eat in. In an increasingly inflationary environment, she manages her grocery bills as part of her budget. Rosie's "Grocery" category covers food she buys at farmer's markets or supermarket chains such as Safeway, Costco, Trader Joe's, etc.

Emily and her husband have three kids. Emily is deeply concerned about climate change and wants to leave a planet for her kids that is safe and habitable. Emily is also passionate about social equity and is a diversity champion at her work. She is interested in spending her capital with organizations that promote sustainable food production practices and employee well-being. Emily pays a premium for buying organic foods while managing her budget. She switches from the traditional grocery definition and creates "Food for Saving the Blue Planet." Who said you couldn't have fun while managing your spending with expense categories? Emily certainly is.

Adam and his partner Levine want to improve their physique and fitness levels. Like Emily, they create a new category, "Fitness Foods." Adam and Levine allocate a budget for "Fitness Foods" to track spending patterns for this category. The "Fitness Foods" categories include protein powders, antioxidant foods like berries, greens, wild-caught salmon, etc. Some may disagree with their definition of fitness foods, but given that Adam and Levine own and develop it they will go far in their goals. Emily, Adam, and Levine are not quiet quitters. They are inquisitive and willing to experiment.

We all deserve better. We can all become better. The uncertainty will never go away. Investing in the self by challenging ourselves is an opportunity to strive toward perfection. And when you are traveling in the maze of life with curiosity and an openness to experiment with habits, you participate in an active, engaged, and enthralling game. Movement, like dancing or shaking to a beat, takes you to the present. So move your hips. Do the cha-cha-cha. Dance to the beat of salsa. This is the game of life. I emphasize that you apply the book's principle of developing your spending categories and sprinkle your personality and preferences all over it. This is the way to State Z. Monks learn to create their own path. Paths others have followed serve as a guide, but there is no feeling more rewarding than walking on a path littered with self-experimentation.

# CHAPTER 10
# DEBT

People get drawn to marketing campaigns with a clear enemy in sight. Food companies have leveraged this strategy on consumers to purchase either fat-free, low carbs, high protein, gluten-free, or many other variations. Political campaigns employ this strategy to get the vote bank out and get increased funding by demonizing taxes, immigrants, inflation, etc. Sports team rivalries create turnouts among the fan base.

We respond to ideas that can be processed with simplicity, and those that we can focus on to gain the upper hand thereby gaining a sense of accomplishment. If you want to conquer an enemy for your financial well-being, and I recommend that you do, take on debt. Debt is the #1 enemy. Taking on this enemy and even fully effacing it will not hurt anyone. Debt is a result of your habits and circumstances. When you can tranquilize this enemy, there is a peace that you will find within. Low or no debt will give you peace of mind that no spa can provide.

The ability to meet your obligations is a sign of responsible behavior. Self-reliance promotes healthy relationships with spouses, happy families, and better careers. People with low or no debt are often risk-takers because they know the fallout from financial decisions. Armed with fact-based information and an attitude that reflects an acute understanding of risk, one can make educated guesses about risk and develop plans to manage it. Managing risk is the pivotal force behind successful entrepreneurship. Warren Buffet, the wealthiest investor in the world, is a gambler who has learned how to take risks in the business world through deliberate and painstaking efforts. Berkshire Hathaway, Mr. Buffett's holding company, owns a diversified portfolio of companies in the banking, consumer goods, energy, insurance, railways, technology, and transportation sectors. Next time you have a delicious nougat from See's Candies, some of those proceeds are landing in Mr. Buffett's bank accounts, proceeds of which are spreading sweetness in more ways than one.

Religious books and great leaders of the past have extolled the virtues of managing debt to preserve liberty for the individual and societies. "The only person who sticks closer to you in adversity than a friend is a creditor." This quote reflects wisdom passed along across cultures.

Unfortunately, the world we live in incentivizes constant selling to the consumer. There has never been so much effort at a mass scale to get the consumer to buy goods and services so well-wrapped with intricate packaging. The packaging is sometimes just literal. For a shameless majority of products and services, it is a figment of the astute advertising industry and boondoggle capitalism to get you to spend money. Not just money that you have today but money that you will earn tomorrow, the day after, next month, and the next year.

Billions flow through the economy focused on studying you, your friends, your relatives, and all of us. Billions are flowing through to find out what will make us spend trillions. In the last twenty years, technology and connectivity have exponentially increased the scale and reach of influence. With the advent of social media, and big data, our spending habits are being studied by large corporations and sold to other interested parties. I recently purchased tires at a tire store with good online reviews. It was my first time visiting this store. Shortly after giving my number at the tire store, I received two text messages, one from a local political candidate and another from a local real estate broker. This is happening across the board. Information is being sold, and potential customers are incessantly targeted.

In addition to the ubiquity of data, your online presence and ability to connect you with the activities of your friends and coworkers, though an admirable technological capability, often result in people comparisons that hinder our quality of life. A friend posting pictures of her boyfriend vacationing in Maldives may trigger feelings of jealousy. Feelings of regret and a sense of missing out are well documented in social media studies. And the compensatory mechanism is the liberal use of credit cards for the next vacation.

I am not advising you to give up your phone or credit cards and become a monk traversing the Himalayas. I use multiple credit cards and a phone and find much value out of these. The key is to manage these devices in our quest for a life of fulfillment and gratitude and not to be sucked into a virtual world that takes away our uniqueness and ability to connect with other people and new experiences. We exhibit freedom when we make choices with our consciousness as decision-makers. It is impractical to be in a state of non-influence; neither is that a healthy mechanism. Learning and growing in life is only possible when we are open to outside influences, and other people and their experiences are great teachers.

Between receiving the influence, and behaving under the influence of an outside force, creating a space for our consciousness to be part of the decision-making is pivotal. Our consciousness tests our judgment and wisdom, allowing critical thinking and choice to guide our decision-making. Self-awareness develops the orchestration layer known colloquially as wisdom. The simple tools in this book intend to ingrain best practices in managing personal finances and expand our self-consciousness to propel us toward the State of Z.

Simple rich people are not immune to the use of credit cards or social media. However, they use it in a prescriptive manner by limiting the usage of these technologies to help further their goals. For example, many simple rich people use WhatsApp to stay connected with family members and friends. However, they do not see the need to spend hours on these technologies or create unproductive habits around them. Simple rich people realize their journey is their own, and though they love to learn about traveling to new places and leverage their resources for traveling tips, they are not in the business of comparing with others. A famous Buddhist saying attributes comparison as the root of human suffering. Theodore Roosevelt penned, "Comparison is the thief of joy." Comparison is a loss-making venture that will steal your money, authenticity, and laughter.

Debt is a worthy enemy. Several financial commentators decry debt and call for its nullification in your life. Though this may sell more books or portray a position that emanates from a monologue worthy of dramatics, this analogy is akin to one that decries fat or carbohydrates in our diet to lose weight. Many scientific studies have shown that a mindful, healthy diet comprised of fats and carbohydrates without deprivation leads to a healthy body weight. Debt provides leverage, and prudent use can significantly increase wealth accumulation. This means that we can reach our financial goals faster. The onus is on the debtor to ensure that debt serves a productive purpose. It is also the responsibility of the debt taker to acquire low-interest debt which can be comfortably paid off.

Financial experts classify debt into two categories: good or healthy debt and bad or unhealthy debt. Don't be fooled into thinking you don't have to repay good debt. You are accountable for paying all of it. Good debt refers to debt used for purchases that have the potential to grow wealth over time. A mortgage loan used to purchase a primary residence is considered good debt. Houses typically appreciate, and we all need a place to live in. Decorating and renovating a home where one enjoys life's special moments is one of the joys of life. The alternative to owning a home is renting. Renting does not offer any tax benefits, and rent does not increase wealth. It's simply a transaction for the tenant to transfer money to a property owner and add to another's wealth.

Generally, only four types of debt are healthy. The first type is student loans that further one's education and future earning potential. The second type is mortgage loans. Homeownership builds assets, equity, and net worth. The third type is necessary medical bills. Finally, debt is often required for building a business to generate future earnings. Education, primary home, essential medical expenditures, and business ventures often constitute good debt. In cardiologists' lingo, these offer "good fat with Omega 3." However, these four categories are not blanket approval for taking on debt. Any debt undertaken must be carefully deliberated.

Alternatives must be explored before taking on any debt, even the healthy kind. An analogy to debt is eating. Eating when hungry is the easiest habit to adopt to live a long life. However, consistently overeating healthy food will also lead to weight gain and related health issues. Debt is the last resort, even for the four categories mentioned above. Creative ideas or alternative decisions often reduce or eliminate the burden of debt.

Sometimes, debt may be unavoidable and worthwhile, such as pursuing a college degree, buying a primary home with a down payment, paying necessary medical bills not covered by insurance, or starting a well-thought-out business venture. However, within these categories, alternatives may reduce the initial debt requirements and even eliminate the need for debt. This could be achieved by lowering the borrowed amount's principal and the borrowed money's interest rate.

College expenditures can be reduced by selecting a more economical college or exploring scholarships more aggressively. Primary home expenditures can be reduced by exploring other homes and locations. Medical expenses can be reduced by exploring jobs with good insurance coverage and changing lifestyle habits such as exercising, avoiding smoking, and substance use. Business debt can be reduced by careful business planning and effective use of resources. A good reputation with money also often leads to help from family and friends who may provide interest-free loans. Once you are an adult, charity offers of no-payment-back loans should never be entertained, not even from your parents or siblings. Your money management reflects your reputation, and money has a hangover effect on the person who borrows and does not repay. It also leaves a bad taste in the mouth of the person who helps and does not get paid back, even if it's your parents or siblings. In all four scenarios, a good credit score will avail you of lower interest rates reducing the overall payments.

Debt for most people is inevitable—a healthy debt with a low-interest rate furthers your life's aspirations. An individual's credit score governs the interest rate. A credit score is like a GPA for financial reputation. Creditors review this score to assess the risk of lending money. The higher the credit scores, the lower the interest rate and overall payments. To determine the impact of debt, a simple calculation measures and reflects on the time spent paying off the debt. This is not intended to avoid taking any debt but to increase awareness of our debt obligations.

Consider Jaime, who is selecting between two computer science programs for undergraduate studies. His options include a private school with a loan of $200,000 and a public school with a loan of $80,000 over four years. Jaime estimates that his pay package will remain the same after graduating from either of the schools. He does prefer the private school with a smaller class size. Jaime does a back-of-the-napkin calculation and estimates that he should be able to pay

$20,000 off the loan every year. The difference in time to pay off debt is four years for public school vs. ten years for private school. This basic calculation does not consider interest rates and is sufficient for Jamie to evaluate his options. Recognizing how much time he would reduce by selecting the public school, he chose the public school and has now graduated and working full time. He also found summer internships at technology companies during his junior and senior year, leaving the college with debts less than he anticipated. After just three years of work, Jaime diligently saved and paid off his student loan debts.

Credit scores impact an individual's ability to borrow money and the loan's interest rate. These three-digit numbers range from zero to eight hundred and affect an individual's ability to rent an apartment, lease a car, or even get a job. Failure to pay credit cards, car loans, home loans, and other payments promptly negatively impacts your credit score. Other variables, such as signing up for many credit cards, may also negatively impact your credit score.

Buying ability is determined by your current financial position, not credit card limits. Credit cards help build a credit history and simplify the buying experience. Convenience comes at a price, however. People spend significantly more on credit cards than on cash. A monthly budgeting process preserves a system of checks and balances on our spending habits. Using credit cards is like using any other tool. It is good to go slow and steady with opening up cards or increasing credit limits, actively monitor the usage and make amends as necessary. Credit card companies make money off the transaction fees paid by the businesses, and are strongly incented to drive consumer spending. The more you spend, the more the industry makes.

In contrast to good or healthy debt, debt in other categories is "bad" or "unhealthy." There may be exceptions in rare cases. Except for well-deliberated, low-interest debt on education, primary mortgage, health, and business ventures, the rest of the obligations will not positively impact your wealth or quality of life in the long run. Purchases of expensive cars, clothes and accessories, vacations, and jewelry will only set you back in terms of your happiness and wealth should they be acquired with debt you cannot afford. A low credit score from reckless purchases will make it harder to procure low-interest-free loans on healthy debt.

When in doubt, three simple questions can help differentiate healthy debt from unhealthy debt. First, ask yourself if the debt you are considering will add value to yourself. For example, a student loan may create opportunities to increase your salary and provide valuable skills for entrepreneurship. Alternatively, a shopping spree for clothing using a credit card will only hurt your finances.

Second, ask yourself if the purchase will appreciate. Buying a primary home would usually pass this test. A vacation home may as well, but I caution you against taking debt for vacation homes. Vacation homes are a luxury and must be paid for with your current financial wherewithal, not a promise to a bank based on your future financial situation. You can leverage a vacation property and mix business with pleasure with rental opportunities like Airbnb, but your modeling must be rooted in reality. Let your creative juices flow on that one. The nomad in me would inquire whether you will be better off exploring the world versus buying a vacation home and tying yourself to just one vacation spot.

Finally, always ask yourself whether you can pay off the debt in a reasonable time and whether that debt will cause you stress. Some people will tell you that money always causes stress. I disagree. From personal experience, I am in a state where money is not a source of botheration. Like most adults, I have bills to pay. I live in San Francisco Bay Area, where affordability is low. I do not recall being stressed about money for several years. And though I do not have car loans, I have a mortgage and a loan for an investment property. I use several credit cards, and neither my property loans nor my credit card balances give me cause for concern. If you are with me in the State of Z, I am incredibly joyous for you, and if you are on the journey, I am very hopeful for you and can't wait to see you.

## Managing Debt

Debt teaches us to be careful of our proclivities and proceed with caution. Debt also teaches self-control and in the process paves the path to liberation. The self-control we develop while learning to manage debt creates discipline in other facets of life, both to develop positive and break harmful habits. There is no limit to the power of self-control. I think of debt less as an enemy and more as a frenemy. Earlier in my financial journey, I viewed debt as the enemy. As I gained wisdom, a better understanding of myself, and a balanced view of personal finance, I realized that debt is a frenemy. Experience with managing debt is an exercise in learning. It's not in my financial interest to vanquish debt but to manage it. Effectively leveraging debt provides a substantial boost toward financial goals.

## Tips for Managing Debt

Money is a leading source of stress for Americans. According to the Stress in America 2022 report by American Psychological Association, inflation was reported as a source of stress for 83% of Americans, and most Americans said the economy (69%) and money (66%) are significant sources of stress.[10] Of the adults who said money is a source of stress, nearly three in five adults (57%) indicated that having money to meet basic needs like rent and mortgage is the primary source of financial stress. Those who report high levels of debt stress suffer from various stress-related illnesses, including ulcers, migraines, back pain, anxiety, depression, and heart attacks.

Multiple research studies have documented the strong connection between financial stressors, marital stress, and health.[11] Financial hardship requires couples to engage in unpleasant resource allocation such as reduced living expenses or finding a second job. Financial stress impacts marital interactions adversely and leads to marital instability. Over time, chronic marital stress can put both parties at risk for developing mental and physical health problems.

Money is the number one issue married couples fight about. Specifically, higher debt leads to fights in marriages. According to Ramsey Solutions' 2017 study, the larger a couple's debt, the more likely money is one of the top issues they fight about. "Almost half (48%) of couples with $50,000 or more in consumer debt say money is a top reason for friction. And those with $50,000 or more in debt were three times more likely than couples with less than $10,000 in debt to say the tone of their money conversations is negative."[12] Debt harms marriages across income levels. 41% of couples with consumer debt say they argue, and it's what they argue about the most. For debt-free couples, money is not even in the top five list of things they argue about. Only 25% of couples who are debt-free quarrel about money. Put another way, three of four couples with no debts do not argue about money at all! Did you feel a pleasant waft of wind breeze through?

Married couples in healthier and happier marriages are more likely to have larger-than-life conversations about their money goals and dreams for a shared future. 87% of respondents classify their marriage as "great" work with their spouse to set their long-term financial goals, compared with 41% who say their marriage is "okay." 94% of those with "great" marriages discuss their dreams together, compared to only 45% of those who self-classified their marriages as "okay" or in "crisis." Money, dreams, and a happy relationship are part of a flywheel that feeds off each other and elevates the spirit of the couples and their families.

A distinguishing characteristic of those who say they have great marriages is their comfort with talking about money with a daily or weekly recurrence. Money is not a source of embarrassment but poise and a segue to their dreams. When discussions about money take place, couples share their emotion about money. Holding on to feelings about money is crippling. Sharing and facing these emotions together builds a partnership of mutual trust and purpose.

A positive relationship with money is synchronous with effectively managing debt. Being open to a relationship's flow while fostering healthy, balanced, and moderate expectations sets a foundation for a positive, long-term relationship. Adopting healthy expectations from the relationship with debt is the foundation of managing it well. To view debt as a necessity versus an avenue for fulfilling our wants, leveraging debt's enablers, such as credit cards, to simplify our lives, and leveraging cheap debt to fast-track the life of our dreams. Adopting these measured expectations will help avoid debt outside your ability to pay comfortably.

In addition to developing expectations, some additional and specific tips follow to manage debt. The first tip is to familiarize yourself with standard credit card terms such as limit and minimum payment. The credit card limit is the total money you can charge to a credit card. All credit cards come with limitations, and available balances are not invitations to splurge. Available credit is not available cash in the bank. It's a loan, and just because you qualify for a loan doesn't mean taking on that responsibility is a good idea.

A commonly misunderstood credit card term is the minimum payment; paying the minimum payment avoids a late payment fee. Paying a minimum balance may avoid late fees by the credit card company, but you will pay high-interest rates on the remaining balance, which will balloon quickly, and the credit card debt can snowball. "According to March 2023 data from the Federal Reserve, the national average credit card APR was 20.09%."[13] Compounding high-interest rates from paying minimum payments can create an untenable and stressful debt position. Owing a large sum of money is like having an old nagging aunt living with you, reminding you constantly of your shortcomings.

Another tip is not to hoard credit options. Having unnecessary open credit cards waiting for a $10 discount to shop at a store or for a rainy day when you'd need plenty of credit to survive creates unnecessary work and is typically not worth the hassle. Most households can leverage three to five good-quality credit cards to access rewards ranging from travel benefits to cash back. Credit card reward seekers can leverage their knowledge of their spending patterns and categories available via budgeting to select cards that will maximize rewards.

Tracking your debt with a regular cadence drives a sense of accomplishment and acts as a warning sign to prevent hitting debt bergs. Debt reduction should be a critical financial goal, and the journey toward managing debt delivers a true sense of freedom and courage to take on challenges in other areas of life. Managing debt effectively is truly an exercise in developing self-belief.

Finally, never throw in the towel. We are all going to face surprise expenses and setbacks. It is part of life's learning. If you are having a bad day or a few bad days, breathe, take a break, and go on a hike. Don't head to a car dealership or an expensive luxury store for watches and handbags. Sometimes, when people fail to pay off their debts, they lose faith in their ability to be financially independent. This is a journey, and you will slip and sometimes fall. And then you will get up. Have faith in your ability to rise.

Return to the basics if you need to catch up on your debts. Do budgeting, reflect on your spending habits, track your debts, and be more cautious next time. But don't throw in the towel. Most people, including myself, have made late payments and interest charges to credit card companies. Most wealthy people have missed car, house, or credit card payments. It didn't stop them from building wealth, nor should it stop you. Debt snowball and debt laddering, two debt reduction strategies, will be shared later in this chapter.

Debt can have adverse physical and psychological impacts. Left unmanaged, mounting debt can sneak up on people. Turning around one's financial situation reflects the growth of character and self-worth. The faster one can spot a spiraling debt situation, the quicker a plan can be made and executed to get out of the rut. Watch out for the indicators below as warning signs:

1. You can only pay part of the monthly balance on the credit card. Minimum payments still accrue interest, and only being able to pay minimum fees is a clear warning sign.

2. You use credit cards to buy necessities like food and gas because of not having the cash to pay for these.

3. You don't know the debts owed and due dates. I am not recommending that you have a number in your head to answer this question extemporaneously at a party. Still, you should know how much you owe and when significant payments are due. Calculate these monthly if you are starting out or early in the process. After this habit is ingrained after tracking for at least three to five years, you may switch to a quarterly cadence.

4. You have to borrow money from friends and family to pay off debts.

5. You start missing payment due dates.

6. Your credit applications get turned down for reasons other than lack of credit.

7. You have creditors contacting you because you are behind in payments.

8. You feel anxious or depressed because of your financial situation.

The last sign is the most telling. It's okay to fall behind; make a plan and start taking small steps to get yourself back to feeling good about how you manage credit. In doing so, you will derive a sense of self-worth and self-confidence.

## Debt Reduction Strategies

There are many different techniques to pay off debt. The best way to pay down debt is whichever method works for you. Many financial experts claim theirs are the best. The ideas have to work for you and your situation. You may not need the two methods that follow. The key takeaway is that there are systematic ways to pay down debt that many before you have successfully applied to achieve peace of mind.

Debt laddering is paying off credit accounts, starting with those accruing the highest interest rates. The interest rates for credit cards are accessible through your monthly statements (the terminology is APR), or you may contact customer service. After reviewing all your credit card accounts and ascertaining the interest rate for each, select the card with the highest interest rate to pay off first. Payments sent to this card should be substantially more than the minimum payment. You should pay the minimum amount on all your other accounts, while the credit card account with the highest interest rate should get as much extra money as possible.

When the account with the highest interest rate is fully paid off, move on to the account with the next highest interest rate. Financial experts who endorse this method suggest that the cards should be closed after you pay them off. Many credit cards enable your access to credit that exceeds your liquidity and incoming income. Each time an account is paid off, move on to the account with the highest interest rate and keep doing so until all the card accounts are paid off.

Debt snowball is another effective debt reduction strategy. When applying the snowball strategy, you start with the account with the smallest balance. And after that, use the smallest balance as the criteria for the subsequent card payments to whittle debt down. The snowball strategy may reduce the debt slower than laddering. However, snowballing can be more gratifying. Quickly paying off to reinstate accounts in good standing is a strong motivator to continue working toward paying off all your debt instead of getting discouraged and giving up.

## Application of Debt Laddering

A sample credit situation is provided below for Marcus's case. With ten credit cards and behind on each, Marcus is at wit's end. His current position is tabulated below.

Marcus's Current Debt Status - December 31, 2021

| # | Card | Interest Rate | Balance | Status |
|---|---|---|---|---|
| 1 | Clothes Retail Card # 1 | 18.99% | $40 | Behind |
| 2 | Clothes Retail Card #2 | 23.99% | $130 | Behind |
| 3 | Online Marketplace Card #1 | 13.24% | $50 | Behind |
| 4 | Electronics Retail Card #1 | 16.50% | $25 | Behind |
| 5 | Supermarket Card #1 | 14.50% | $80 | Behind |
| 6 | Supermarket Card #2 | 17.50% | $35 | Behind |
| 7 | Game Retail #1 | 19.28% | $65 | Behind |
| 8 | Juice Bar Card #1 | 22.99% | $95 | Behind |
| 9 | Shoes Store Card #1 | 17.32% | $75 | Behind |
| 10 | Coffee Chain Card #1 | 15.99% | $5 | Behind |
| | Total Debt | | $600 | |

"Font Index: Red (Behind), Blue (Progress made in reducing dues, but still behind), Green (Payments made on time)"

Marcus reads about these two debt reduction strategies online. He prefers laddering for its expediency and is committed to saving and contributing $100 monthly to reduce his credit card debt. For simplicity of calculations, the below examples do not include interest rate penalties.

After the first month, Marcus pays off minimum balances on all credit cards and then an additional $100 to reduce the balance on Clothes Retail Card #2, which accrues the highest interest rate of 23.99%. He is still behind by $30 but has saved interest charges on the $100 and is getting closer to getting on track for payments on this card. His debt position at the end of January is tabulated below.

Marcus's Debt Status - January 31, 2022 (Debt Laddering)

| # | Card | Interest Rate | Previous Balance | Current Balance | Status |
|---|------|---------------|------------------|-----------------|--------|
| 1 | Clothes Retail Card # 1 | 18.99% | $40 | $40 | Behind |
| 2 | Clothes Retail Card #2 | 23.99% | $130 | $30 | Behind |
| 3 | Online Marketplace Card #1 | 13.24% | $50 | $50 | Behind |
| 4 | Electronics Retail Card #1 | 16.50% | $25 | $25 | Behind |
| 5 | Supermarket Card #1 | 14.50% | $80 | $80 | Behind |
| 6 | Supermarket Card #2 | 17.50% | $35 | $35 | Behind |
| 7 | Game Retail #1 | 19.28% | $65 | $65 | Behind |
| 8 | Juice Bar Card #1 | 22.99% | $95 | $95 | Behind |
| 9 | Shoes Store Card #1 | 17.32% | $75 | $75 | Behind |
| 10 | Coffee Chain Card #1 | 15.99% | $5 | $5 | Behind |
| | Total Debt | | $600 | $500 | |

The following month, Marcus is on track for Clothes Retail Card #2 and making inroads with Juice Bar Card #1, the card with the next highest interest rate. His debt position at the end of February is tabulated below.

Marcus's Debt Status - February 28, 2022 (Debt Laddering)

| # | Card | Interest Rate | Previous Balance | Current Balance | Status |
|---|------|---------------|------------------|-----------------|--------|
| 1 | Clothes Retail Card # 1 | 18.99% | $40 | $40 | Behind |
| 2 | Clothes Retail Card #2 | 23.99% | $30 | $0 | Current |
| 3 | Online Marketplace Card #1 | 13.24% | $50 | $50 | Behind |
| 4 | Electronics Retail Card #1 | 16.50% | $25 | $25 | Behind |
| 5 | Supermarket Card #1 | 14.50% | $80 | $80 | Behind |
| 6 | Supermarket Card #2 | 17.50% | $35 | $35 | Behind |
| 7 | Game Retail #1 | 19.28% | $65 | $65 | Behind |
| 8 | Juice Bar Card #1 | 22.99% | $95 | $25 | Behind |
| 9 | Shoes Store Card #1 | 17.32% | $75 | $75 | Behind |
| 10 | Coffee Chain Card #1 | 15.99% | $5 | $5 | Behind |
|  | Total Debt |  | $500 | $400 |  |

At the end of the third month of applying the debt laddering strategy, Marcus is paying on time with three cards and making progress with the fourth. His debt position at the end of March is tabulated below.

Marcus's Debt Status - March 31, 2022 (Debt Laddering)

| # | Card | Interest Rate | Previous Balance | Current Balance | Status |
|---|---|---|---|---|---|
| 1 | Clothes Retail Card # 1 | 18.99% | $40 | $30 | Behind |
| 2 | Clothes Retail Card #2 | 23.99% | $0 | $0 | Current |
| 3 | Online Marketplace Card #1 | 13.24% | $50 | $50 | Behind |
| 4 | Electronics Retail Card #1 | 16.50% | $25 | $25 | Behind |
| 5 | Supermarket Card #1 | 14.50% | $80 | $80 | Behind |
| 6 | Supermarket Card #2 | 17.50% | $35 | $35 | Behind |
| 7 | Game Retail #1 | 19.28% | $65 | $0 | Current |
| 8 | Juice Bar Card #1 | 22.99% | $25 | $0 | Current |
| 9 | Shoes Store Card #1 | 17.32% | $75 | $75 | Behind |
| 10 | Coffee Chain Card #1 | 15.99% | $5 | $5 | Behind |
| | Total Debt | | $400 | $300 | |

"Font Index: Red (Behind), Blue (Progress made in reducing dues, but still behind), Green (Payments made on time)"

After only four months, Marcus has erased the backlog of five credit cards, half of all his open credit cards. His debt position at the end of April, May, and June are tabulated below.

Marcus's Debt Status - April 30, 2022 (Debt Laddering)

| # | Card | Interest Rate | Previous Balance | Current Balance | Status |
|---|---|---|---|---|---|
| 1 | Clothes Retail Card # 1 | 18.99% | $30 | $0 | Current |
| 2 | Clothes Retail Card #2 | 23.99% | $0 | $0 | Current |
| 3 | Online Marketplace Card #1 | 13.24% | $50 | $50 | Behind |
| 4 | Electronics Retail Card #1 | 16.50% | $25 | $25 | Behind |
| 5 | Supermarket Card #1 | 14.50% | $80 | $80 | Behind |
| 6 | Supermarket Card #2 | 17.50% | $35 | $0 | Current |
| 7 | Game Retail #1 | 19.28% | $0 | $0 | Current |
| 8 | Juice Bar Card #1 | 22.99% | $0 | $0 | Current |
| 9 | Shoes Store Card #1 | 17.32% | $75 | $40 | Behind |
| 10 | Coffee Chain Card #1 | 15.99% | $5 | $5 | Behind |
| | Total Debt | | $300 | $200 | |

"Font Index: Red (Behind), Blue (Progress made in reducing dues, but still behind), Green (Payments made on time)"

## Marcus's Debt Status - May 31, 2022 (Debt Laddering)

| # | Card | Interest Rate | Previous Balance | Current Balance | Status |
|---|------|---------------|------------------|-----------------|--------|
| 1 | Clothes Retail Card # 1 | 18.99% | $0 | $0 | Behind |
| 2 | Clothes Retail Card #2 | 23.99% | $0 | $0 | Current |
| 3 | Online Marketplace Card #1 | 13.24% | $50 | $50 | Behind |
| 4 | Electronics Retail Card #1 | 16.50% | $25 | $0 | Current |
| 5 | Supermarket Card #1 | 14.50% | $80 | $50 | Behind |
| 6 | Supermarket Card #2 | 17.50% | $0 | $0 | Current |
| 7 | Game Retail #1 | 19.28% | $0 | $0 | Current |
| 8 | Juice Bar Card #1 | 22.99% | $0 | $0 | Current |
| 9 | Shoes Store Card #1 | 17.32% | $40 | $0 | Current |
| 10 | Coffee Chain Card #1 | 15.99% | $5 | $0 | Current |
|  | Total Debt |  | $200 | $100 |  |

"Font Index: Red (Behind), Blue (Progress made in reducing dues, but still behind), Green (Payments made on time)"

Marcus's Debt Status - June 30, 2022 (Debt Laddering)

| # | Card | Interest Rate | Previous Balance | Current Balance | Status |
|---|------|--------------|------------------|-----------------|--------|
| 1 | Clothes Retail Card # 1 | 18.99% | $0 | $0 | Behind |
| 2 | Clothes Retail Card #2 | 23.99% | $0 | $0 | Current |
| 3 | Online Marketplace Card #1 | 13.24% | $50 | $0 | Current |
| 4 | Electronics Retail Card #1 | 16.50% | $0 | $0 | Current |
| 5 | Supermarket Card #1 | 14.50% | $50 | $0 | Current |
| 6 | Supermarket Card #2 | 17.50% | $0 | $0 | Current |
| 7 | Game Retail #1 | 19.28% | $0 | $0 | Current |
| 8 | Juice Bar Card #1 | 22.99% | $0 | $0 | Current |
| 9 | Shoes Store Card #1 | 17.32% | $0 | $0 | Current |
| 10 | Coffee Chain Card #1 | 15.99% | $0 | $0 | Current |
|  | Total Debt |  | $100 | $0 |  |

"Font Index: Red (Behind), Blue (Progress made in reducing dues, but still behind), Green (Payments made on time)"

After only six months of applying the laddering method, Marcus is up to date on all his credit card accounts. Marcus feels proud about his progress and now strategically reviews his card accounts. Looking at his usage and purchase patterns, Marcus closes all credit cards except Online Marketplace Card #1 and Supermarket Card #1. In addition, he gets a new credit card not affiliated with any stores that give him 2% cash back off any purchases and 3% cash back for any gas purchases. He plans to use this card for all purchases except when he shops at Marketplace #1 and Supermarket #1. His final tally for credit cards is tabulated below. By reducing the number of credit cards by 70%, Marcus is spending strategically and maximizing value. He has also simplified his life and administrative burden for managing ten cards.

And by clipping available credit he is systemically placing guardrails to prevent him from spending more than his means.

Marcus's Debt Status - After Strategic Review

| # | Card | Interest Rate | Status |
|---|------|---------------|--------|
| 3 | Online Marketplace Card #1 | 13.24% | Current |
| 5 | Supermarket Card #1 | 14.50% | Current |
| 10 | High Rewards Credit Card | 21.99% | Current |
| | Total Debt | | |

"Font Index: Red (Behind), Blue (Progress made in reducing dues, but still behind), Green (Payments made on time)"

## Application of Debt Snowball

Marcus could have also used debt snowball as a strategy to pay down debt. This strategy focuses on paying off debt with the lowest balance, irrespective of the interest rates, gaining momentum as you knock out each remaining balance. To illustrate, Marcus's starting position at the end of 2021 is below.

## Marcus's Current Debt Status - December 31, 2021

| # | Card | Interest Rate | Balance | Status |
|---|------|---------------|---------|--------|
| 1 | Clothes Retail Card # 1 | 18.99% | $40 | Behind |
| 2 | Clothes Retail Card #2 | 23.99% | $130 | Behind |
| 3 | Online Marketplace Card #1 | 13.24% | $50 | Behind |
| 4 | Electronics Retail Card #1 | 16.50% | $25 | Behind |
| 5 | Supermarket Card #1 | 14.50% | $80 | Behind |
| 6 | Supermarket Card #2 | 17.50% | $35 | Behind |
| 7 | Game Retail #1 | 19.28% | $65 | Behind |
| 8 | Juice Bar Card #1 | 22.99% | $95 | Behind |
| 9 | Shoes Store Card #1 | 17.32% | $75 | Behind |
| 10 | Coffee Chain Card #1 | 15.99% | $5 | Behind |
| | Total Debt | | $600 | |

"Font Index: Red (Behind), Blue (Progress made in reducing dues, but still behind), Green (Payments made on time)"

After Marcus pays off his minimum balance on all cards, he pays an extra $100 each month to pay off credit card debt starting with the card with the lowest debt amount. As illustrated below, in just the first month Marcus has caught up with three credit cards and making progress with the fourth one! Even though laddering leads to lower overall outlays, snowball creates momentum and reduces calls from the tenacious and pesky debt collectors.

## Marcus's Debt Status - January 31, 2022 (Debt Snowball)

| # | Card | Interest Rate | Previous Balance | Current Balance | Status |
|---|------|---------------|------------------|-----------------|--------|
| 1 | Clothes Retail Card # 1 | 18.99% | $40 | $5 | Behind |
| 2 | Clothes Retail Card #2 | 23.99% | $130 | $130 | Current |
| 3 | Online Marketplace Card #1 | 13.24% | $50 | $50 | Behind |
| 4 | Electronics Retail Card #1 | 16.50% | $25 | $0 | Current |
| 5 | Supermarket Card #1 | 14.50% | $80 | $80 | Behind |
| 6 | Supermarket Card #2 | 17.50% | $35 | $0 | Current |
| 7 | Game Retail #1 | 19.28% | $65 | $65 | Behind |
| 8 | Juice Bar Card #1 | 22.99% | $95 | $95 | Behind |
| 9 | Shoes Store Card #1 | 17.32% | $75 | $75 | Behind |
| 10 | Coffee Chain Card #1 | 15.99% | $5 | $0 | Current |
| | Total Debt | | $600 | $500 | |

"Font Index: Red (Behind), Blue (Progress made in reducing dues, but still behind), Green (Payments made on time)"

At the end of the second month, Marcus paid off his debt balance on five cards and made progress on the sixth. In just two months, Marcus has made significant progress in managing his debt and improving his peace of mind. Marcus can share his plan when the remaining four credit card companies call him inquiring. He should also ask if they can waive any interest penalties.

## Marcus's Debt Status - February 28, 2022 (Debt Snowball)

| # | Card | Interest Rate | Previous Balance | Current Balance | Status |
|---|------|---------------|------------------|-----------------|--------|
| 1 | Clothes Retail Card # 1 | 18.99% | $5 | $0 | Current |
| 2 | Clothes Retail Card #2 | 23.99% | $130 | $130 | Behind |
| 3 | Online Marketplace Card #1 | 13.24% | $50 | $0 | Current |
| 4 | Electronics Retail Card #1 | 16.50% | $0 | $0 | Current |
| 5 | Supermarket Card #1 | 14.50% | $80 | $80 | Behind |
| 6 | Supermarket Card #2 | 17.50% | $0 | $0 | Current |
| 7 | Game Retail #1 | 19.28% | $65 | $20 | Behind |
| 8 | Juice Bar Card #1 | 22.99% | $95 | $95 | Behind |
| 9 | Shoes Store Card #1 | 17.32% | $75 | $75 | Behind |
| 10 | Coffee Chain Card #1 | 15.99% | $0 | $0 | Current |
|  | Total Debt |  | $500 | $400 |  |

"Font Index: Red (Behind), Blue (Progress made in reducing dues, but still behind), Green (Payments made on time)"

As illustrated below, using the debt snowball method, Marcus pays off in six months with the last credit card taking two months to pay, the mirror example of debt laddering in which the first credit card took two months to pay off. Either method will work wonders for your debt and your happiness.

## Marcus's Debt Status - March 31, 2022 (Debt Snowball)

| # | Card | Interest Rate | Previous Balance | Current Balance | Status |
|---|------|---------------|------------------|-----------------|--------|
| 1 | Clothes Retail Card # 1 | 18.99% | $0 | $0 | Current |
| 2 | Clothes Retail Card #2 | 23.99% | $130 | $130 | Behind |
| 3 | Online Marketplace Card #1 | 13.24% | $0 | $0 | Current |
| 4 | Electronics Retail Card #1 | 16.50% | $0 | $0 | Current |
| 5 | Supermarket Card #1 | 14.50% | $80 | $75 | Behind |
| 6 | Supermarket Card #2 | 17.50% | $0 | $0 | Current |
| 7 | Game Retail #1 | 19.28% | $20 | $0 | Current |
| 8 | Juice Bar Card #1 | 22.99% | $95 | $95 | Behind |
| 9 | Shoes Store Card #1 | 17.32% | $75 | $0 | Current |
| 10 | Coffee Chain Card #1 | 15.99% | $0 | $0 | Current |
| | Total Debt | | $400 | $300 | |

"Font Index: Red (Behind), Blue (Progress made in reducing dues, but still behind), Green (Payments made on time)"

## Marcus's Debt Status - April 30, 2022 (Debt Snowball)

| # | Card | Interest Rate | Previous Balance | Current Balance | Status |
|---|------|---------------|------------------|-----------------|--------|
| 1 | Clothes Retail Card # 1 | 18.99% | $0 | $0 | Current |
| 2 | Clothes Retail Card #2 | 23.99% | $130 | $130 | Behind |
| 3 | Online Marketplace Card #1 | 13.24% | $0 | $0 | Current |
| 4 | Electronics Retail Card #1 | 16.50% | $0 | $0 | Current |
| 5 | Supermarket Card #1 | 14.50% | $75 | $0 | Current |
| 6 | Supermarket Card #2 | 17.50% | $0 | $0 | Current |
| 7 | Game Retail #1 | 19.28% | $0 | $0 | Current |
| 8 | Juice Bar Card #1 | 22.99% | $95 | $70 | Behind |
| 9 | Shoes Store Card #1 | 17.32% | $0 | $0 | Current |
| 10 | Coffee Chain Card #1 | 15.99% | $0 | $0 | Current |
| | Total Debt | | $300 | $200 | |

"Font Index: Red (Behind), Blue (Progress made in reducing dues, but still behind), Green (Payments made on time)"

## Marcus's Debt Status - May 31, 2022 (Debt Snowball)

| # | Card | Interest Rate | Previous Balance | Current Balance | Status |
|---|------|---------------|------------------|-----------------|--------|
| 1 | Clothes Retail Card # 1 | 18.99% | $0 | $0 | Current |
| 2 | Clothes Retail Card #2 | 23.99% | $130 | $100 | Behind |
| 3 | Online Marketplace Card #1 | 13.24% | $0 | $0 | Current |
| 4 | Electronics Retail Card #1 | 16.50% | $0 | $0 | Current |
| 5 | Supermarket Card #1 | 14.50% | $0 | $0 | Current |
| 6 | Supermarket Card #2 | 17.50% | $0 | $0 | Current |
| 7 | Game Retail #1 | 19.28% | $0 | $0 | Current |
| 8 | Juice Bar Card #1 | 22.99% | $70 | $0 | Current |
| 9 | Shoes Store Card #1 | 17.32% | $0 | $0 | Current |
| 10 | Coffee Chain Card #1 | 15.99% | $0 | $0 | Current |
| | Total Debt | | $200 | $100 | |

"Font Index: Red (Behind), Blue (Progress made in reducing dues, but still behind), Green (Payments made on time)"

## Marcus's Debt Status - June 30, 2022 (Debt Snowball)

| # | Card | Interest Rate | Previous Balance | Current Balance | Status |
|---|------|--------------|------------------|-----------------|--------|
| 1 | Clothes Retail Card # 1 | 18.99% | $0 | $0 | Current |
| 2 | Clothes Retail Card #2 | 23.99% | $100 | $0 | Current |
| 3 | Online Marketplace Card #1 | 13.24% | $0 | $0 | Current |
| 4 | Electronics Retail Card #1 | 16.50% | $0 | $0 | Current |
| 5 | Supermarket Card #1 | 14.50% | $0 | $0 | Current |
| 6 | Supermarket Card #2 | 17.50% | $0 | $0 | Current |
| 7 | Game Retail #1 | 19.28% | $0 | $0 | Current |
| 8 | Juice Bar Card #1 | 22.99% | $0 | $0 | Current |
| 9 | Shoes Store Card #1 | 17.32% | $0 | $0 | Current |
| 10 | Coffee Chain Card #1 | 15.99% | $0 | $0 | Current |
| | Total Debt | | $100 | $0 | |

"Font Index: Red (Behind), Blue (Progress made in reducing dues, but still behind), Green (Payments made on time)"

## Debt Epilogue

Simple rich people avoid unnecessary debt, like most people avoid the dentist. Simple rich people see debt as a potential hazard to their physical and mental well-being and carefully manage it. The tools they use are straightforward. They are measuring debt on a monthly or quarterly frequency, ensuring that credit cards are working to streamline their lives and simplify their purchases. There are plenty of challenges in life, from unconscionable bosses at work, backstabbing coworkers, kid's stressors, and nagging aunts. Having manageable debt provides a thick armor for life's twists and turns.

Debt is personal for simple rich people. Simple rich people view excessive debt as a reflection of their habits. Simple rich people are concerned about profligacy, not just in themselves but in their societies. I have often found simple rich people have a sense of fairness that reflects a code of ethics. The core value of simplicity extends to their time management as well. Simple rich people trust their ingenuity to manage their time optimally and continue to invest in their learning to satisfy their curiosity to keep improving their lives and those around them.

# CHAPTER 11
# MONEY AND RELATIONSHIPS

Money has a significant bearing on relationships. It is sad to come across the oft-prevalent occurrences of siblings, who shared precious moments of innocence as kids together, ending up squabbling over their parents' belongings or a shared piece of real estate. It is unsettling to find people burning bonds for fiat money. Money is simply a resource to help with living a fulfilling life. As the hammer eventually falls on our lives, memories, not money, provide meaning and satisfaction. In the movie classic Citizen Kane, Charles Kane recalls his beloved toy sled as he passes into nothingness.

Simple rich people recognize the value of money as a determinant of their quality of life. They acknowledge that money is a resource and productive personal finance habits can increase their pot of gold. However, they are careful not to draw their intrinsic self-worth from how much they have. Neither do they compare with another, whether friends or siblings or someone they met at a party. Simple rich people inculcate an appreciation of others' possessions. If simple rich people see a collectible art painting at a house party, they appreciate the beauty. It is not that they are not aware that the owner must have doled out some significant cash to acquire the masterpiece they admire. But that is a realization and no more. They do not need to feel deficient because of someone else's possessions. Every once in a while, when they feel jealous, they can accept their feelings and course correct. This prevents simple rich people from acting on those feelings. Several simple rich people often feel a sense of relief that they are enjoying the experience of the classier things in life without worrying about the acquisition and maintenance overhead. Simple rich people may often see possessions they are not keenly interested in as potential distractions from their true calling.

This is a secret to their happiness, and discipline. Buddha said, "Comparison is the root of all human suffering." If they meet with someone whose car and house are a lot more expensive than theirs, they appreciate the car and the house with the air of a television chef eating a delicacy made by the show contestants. They will savor it, smell the roses, and even appreciate their good fortune to access a positive experience.

After dining with a simple rich friend, we strolled around his neighborhood. As we walked, he told me about his neighbor's car-buying patterns and home-remodeling projects. There were the typical luxury brands in an upscale American suburb. The Teslas, the Mercedes, the Beamers. A couple of homes were also getting significant remodeling. As he walked around, I noticed the excitement in his voice as he described his neighbors' properties. This was quite the reverse effect of "Keeping Up with the Joneses." His attitude reflected "Highlighting the Joneses" or "Showcasing the Joneses." After driving a Honda Accord for much of his adult life, he had recently purchased a second-hand Audi. While he was pretty excited by other people's investments in their homes, he has to be nudged repeatedly by his wife to make any progress on his home improvement projects, which happens relatively infrequently. When I inquired on this conundrum, he told me quite earnestly that when his neighbors livened up their homes and purchased luxury cars, he was pleased for them because they were hopefully employing capital to enrich their lifestyle. Further, he added that his neighbors' investments improved the neighborhood ambience, and increased the neighborhood's market value, including his home's. Though idiosyncratic, it's hard to argue with a strategy that increases your net worth without any personal investment!

Not comparing one's possessions and not judging worth by material possessions promotes productive and empathetic relationships. Simple rich people bring this emotional maturity to their relationships as a parent, sibling, friend, or coworker. Their ability to neither evaluate a person's worth by material possessions nor compare builds trust and respect. Their friends and relations highly solicit their unbiased advice. Simple rich people are treated with respect and dignity because they are fair in their dealings. Armed with gratitude and an armor of kindness, simple rich people demonstrate integrity and are often invited to moderate disputes.

Simple rich people view money as simply a resource. A resource that can be leveraged to protect their way of life. They do not attach their worth to how much they have but pay attention to their financial and personal growth. They do not value others better or worse simply because of a few pieces of fiat paper at their disposal. Simple rich people value character and integrity. Happiness and courage reflect the journey undertaken, not where you reach at the end. However, they understand that the future will typically be much further if the journey has been one of courage, tenacity, and self-reflection.

Simple rich people are careful not to let money intrude in relationships. They do so by paying their share to their friends, families, and society. Not just a percentage of their money but their share in the burden of our collective lives. As they chart and assert their independence and protect their way of life, they also take pains not to encroach on the lives of others. Their care and kindness result in meaningful relationships. It's the shining of their character that endears people to them. Their simplicity is charming, authenticity is infectious, and their way of life is humble.

Simple rich people create a system in their family networks to drive growth. They encourage their kids to learn and grow and avoid excessive shows of wealth. Their children are taught early on not just with empty words but by actions about the benefits of living below their means. The kids learn by seeing their parents that a life of peace, harmony, and learning is prioritized over besting others socially through material pursuits. Simple rich people work hard to create an environment where their kids can access opportunities but are not entitled to them. They also try to pass on the values of a successful life and leave the specifics of the path to the children. They know from their experience the struggles and joys of building your own path and see this as the quintessential atom for a successful life.

As simple rich people grow, their focus expands organically and intentionally to influence society. Work never stops. They take pauses and vacations, reenergize themselves but recognize that work and life go hand in hand. It is not that they are simply workhorses just working to pass the time. It is their insatiable desire to learn and grow and recognition that the path to learn and grow passes through the woods of work. They encourage others in society to follow the path of assiduousness through their behaviors.

The defining quality of simple rich people that helps them live lives of purpose and build long-term, respectful relationships is acceptance. Acceptance of self, acceptance of others around them, and most importantly acceptance of the systems that create the behaviors of the people within them. However, it is not passive acceptance. This acceptance is complemented by passive resistance, which helps simple rich people ground themselves in reality and continue struggling for a better state. The complementarity of these attributes, the yin and the yang, propel simple rich people to attain the State of Z.

# CHAPTER 12

# WEALTH IN A WOMAN'S WORLD

Significant progress has been made in the last hundred years in improving the welfare of women. Women are joining the workforce in record numbers. Though there are occasional setbacks in parts of the world, such as the treatment of women in Afghanistan under the Taliban or the attack on reproductive rights by the American Taliban, women have made great strides toward owning their destiny during the last hundred years. Women have a more significant say in their homes. Women are choosing to love and marry who they feel like. Women are choosing to be single and to express themselves freely. Women contribute to and lead branches of service they were previously "sheltered" from. Women have been transformational CEOs of their houses before; now they lead the organizations providing goods and services to these households. Women's perceptions and intuition are changing how companies operate. Women are feeling less suffocated and are setting an example for human progress and as a liberating light for the oppressed.

Women are not alone in this struggle. Men of all backgrounds and those from other genders are active partners in their strides. Women are not simply growing in a vacuum. Men are making strides in growth as well. This is not to take away the credit from women's rights movements. Progress is always made in tandem with others living in society. Men have been partners in the progress. Many grandfathers, fathers, brothers, uncles, mentors, colleagues, sons, sons-in-law, and bosses have been rooting for removing shackles from women so they can experience a life of dignity and growth. Women and their partners in society are breaking down archaic societal systems that prevent a woman from learning and developing.

Other struggles, such as those for minorities and LGBTQ causes, complement the effort for women's rights. Liberty and justice movements for any group are partners in liberating humanity from our biases and egocentric worldviews.

The 20th century was a layup for the liberation of women and societies. The 21st century will be markedly the women's century. The last seventy-five years have seen more progress for women on a global scale than any time before. Women are on course to contribute and deliver a profound and positive impact in politics, society, and business in the current century. The positive trajectory for women's progress is a shared sentiment by many men, who do not wish gender to hinder the achievements of their daughters, wives, friends, and coworkers. Many business leaders, irrespective of gender, are authentically pushing for opportunities for women in the workforce because it is not only an ethical way to conduct business but a sensible way. Excluding or marginalizing half of the talent, especially a group hungry for change, and which brings a novel and diverse perspective for connecting with customers and business stakeholders, is a surefire way to downgrade talent and give up market share.

Women bring empathy and compassion to the workplace, which also benefits men. Would men have ever benefited from paternity leave without maternity leave being in place? A few decades ago, family-friendly policies at work were viewed as going soft, or in classical corporate speak, "unfashionable subjects." Today's business thinking promotes employee well-being. Business leaders recognize the link between employees' workplace productivity and employee well-being. Organizations increasingly focus on programs and facilities supporting the employee's holistic needs.

Organizations have implemented policies to encourage women to return to work after maternity. Women have continued to gain confidence and become impatient with organizational cultures that cannot deliver career growth opportunities. Kudos! In McKinsey's 2022 Woman in the Workplace report, women leaders are switching jobs at the highest rates, and ambitious young women are prepared to do the same.[14] Women are also graduating, in increasing numbers from colleges. In the 2018-19 academic year, over 1.1 million women received a bachelor's degree compared to fewer than 860,000 men. That's one hundred new women graduates for seventy-four men graduates. Women outperforming men is a consistent trend across higher education levels, including associate and master's degrees. Companies and managers that are impervious to the growing aspirations of women and the changing dynamics in the talent pool are eroding their competitive advantage.

This societal change is impacting not only the futures of companies but that of countries as well. Countries that have opened up the labor force and actioning women's rights have markedly better economies, more open and diverse societies, and offer a better quality of life. It is not simply enough for women to participate in the workforce but to have equal opportunities at all levels, especially at higher levels of income and power. Several countries have high levels of female participation in plantation work and low-paying jobs while they also bear the burden of childbearing and child-rearing. It's not a matter of simply quantity. The quality of work and the spectrum of power women exert determines the quality of life for societies, families, and the individual. Women's experience influences the next generation's expectations of themselves and their partners and has far-reaching consequences for social structures and relationships.

The changing power structures significantly affect men's quality of life, including men's primal need to mate and pass on their genes to the next generation. College-educated women seek mates who are not only college educated but also supportive of women in their careers. After the relationship starts, these same traits also determine the longevity and quality of the relationship.

Men interested in having long-term relationships with competent, successful women should ideally develop genes to gain an evolutionary advantage. The development of pragmatic money management and partner-centric habits comes a close second. Money and security have always been a critical criterion for selecting mates. It continues to be, and men better at managing money have an advantage going into this competition. This road goes two ways. Successful men are not eager to get married to debt-ridden partners.

According to Ramsey System's study on money, marriage, and communication conducted in 2017, money is the number one issue couples fight about.12 The higher a couple's debt burden, the more likely they are to argue about money. Couples in healthy marriages feel comfortable sharing their aspirations about money and long-term goals. No couple gets money right 100% of the time, and almost all couples face financial struggles as part of their marital life. The couples' expression of vulnerability to discuss their past and share dreams about their future helps create a bond of trust and shared aspirations.

Security for their families and independence for the self is highly prized by most women, regardless of their marital status or sexual orientation. Getting adept at effective money management provides women the resources to live their own lives without compromising their true selves and dreams. A young woman reading this book under a palm tree and applying principles to grow and develop into a simple rich woman would be the best gift for this guide.

# CHAPTER 13

# AI: THE NEW FRONTIER

Since I started writing this book a year ago, ChatGPT, an advanced form of artificial intelligence (AI), has come to the forefront. In this chapter, I will often use ChatGPT and AI interchangeably. Business leaders view the conversational ability of ChatGPT as a gold mine to improve business outcomes and transform business management and resource allocation. Common people are embracing it with gusto as well. ChatGPT has a plethora of information and conversational and analytical skills that mirror human interactions. People are eagerly embracing the nascent technology to plan their travel, learn about new technologies, create business emails, and documents.

It is hard to predict the specific impacts of this groundbreaking and potent technology, but what is certain is its widespread influence and competitive differentiation across industries and households. Productivity gains will be immense for the companies and governments that invest in AI thoughtfully. AI will also provide a medium for individuals to quickly grasp concepts accelerating a democratization of information and knowledge.

However, there is an uncomfortable truth. The technology will create winners and losers, likely exacerbating income and wealth inequality. Office jobs will be subject to change, and many will be replaced. Outsourcing manufacturing led to significant job losses; AI will do the same at a much larger scale. On the flip side, AI will also create immense opportunities to reinvigorate careers, develop new products and services, and elevate the quality of life at work and in personal life.

Within the next few years, AI will change the future of work and how people learn, live, and communicate in a rapidly evolving fashion. Governments, businesses, households, and individuals will be able to harness the power of AI. It is of universal interest to incorporate AI into our daily lives. Just like electricity powered work later into the night, powering subsequent innovations, AI is opening pathways to new ways of working. The quantum leap gained by human beings allows accessible learning, incubation of new products and services, and an opportunity for those without significant resources to build a self-reliant life. These benefits will not come without pain. Many jobs will be replaced, while others will be attuned to a greater interaction with AI technologies. The effects, especially in office settings, will be significant and change will bring about stress – a change that will reverberate across industries.

This may seem like a Stephen King book where robots are coming for your jobs and way of life, and there is nowhere to hide creating an unsettling feeling of helplessness and despair. However, there is a promising outlook for how AI can improve life quality. This outlook is projected from a repetition of the history of technology-induced positive impact, accelerated by the advent of personal computing.

Personal computing became ubiquitous and broadened access to technology for individuals and households starting in the 80s. Computing investments improved business productivity, and individuals and households started using basic document generation, spreadsheet, and database programs and enjoying video games. The 90s broadened technology and connectivity access with the mass adoption of the internet. Software and hardware investments in the business and personal space improved productivity and created a whole new e-commerce sector. New companies such as Amazon and eBay came into play, revolutionizing the way products were sold. These portals also provided opportunities to many entrepreneurs who could now sell from their homes and broaden access to their products and services.

E-commerce brought new opportunities but also decimated many businesses and transformed many others. Netflix transformed the media business, and Amazon transformed the retail business starting with revolutionizing the purchases of books. Access to knowledge broadened, democratizing information, creating a greater meritocracy. Then came the mobility revolution changing how consumers and businesses produce and consume information. Mobile phones, now in ubiquitous use globally and embraced by all strata in society, allowed people to be connected on the go and revolutionized business operations and consumer lives. Organizations adapted to expand outreach and connect with consumers. Many other developments continued to transform interactions and consumer preferences. Social media, cloud computing, blockchain, cryptocurrency, Internet of things, virtual reality, ERP software. The list goes on. These technologies have been the precursor for Artificial Intelligence, the next transformative technology.

The brief history of technology showcases people, businesses, and societies grappling with and leveraging technologies. The trajectory of the application of technology has been increasing, and so has the rate of change. Artificial intelligence is a natural milestone for technological advancements, and owing to some brilliant, forward-thinking individuals it's at our fingertips to transform our lives.

The experience of booking a vacation illustrates this. Consumers can book tickets comparing various sites, and travelers select hotels and activities by reading feedback. Most hotels advertise their proximity to tourist attractions, and user feedback provides a gauge for selecting these hotels. Many vloggers and regular tourists share their experiences and travelers can get a sneak peek of the places they plan to visit and many other helpful tips including the time to go, city passes, restaurants, etc. And now, with advances in AI, one can solicit input from ChatGPT to plan a trip. Inputs can be customized to incorporate the requestor's preferences. "Suggest an itinerary for three days in Paris for a family of four with kids 5 and 12." "Suggest an itinerary for four days in Durban for a couple. We love museums and attending sports events."

Compare this with the pre-internet days when one would need to hire a travel agent and make phone calls to hotels and peruse travel guidebooks the size of a full-length novel. Often, the effort itself and the risk of the unknown would be a deterrent to travel. With technology, the tourism industry has come ahead along with economic well-being for many locals who have been able to find gainful employment. Most importantly, people are better traveled and gain an appreciation of other cultures, building a connected world. It would be remiss not to point out that the jobs of travel agents have been impacted by technology. Many travel agencies thrived by focusing on a niche customer base, leveraging technologies to make their delivery more resonant with their client base and offering more choice. Other travel agents who may not have been able to adapt have been able to port their skill set of customer service and relationship building to other jobs and new ventures. However, this transition would have been a learning experience. The attitude with which we face technology is a differentiator in the outcome. We do not have a vote concerning technological advancement, and the pervasiveness of technology. Nonetheless, we have an absolute choice to embrace new technologies, and that's all that matters.

Since the 1980s, technologies have radically changed our lives. The aphorism "change is the only constant" resonates ever more vividly. Being financially self-reliant is a key support system in our ability to tackle adverse impacts from technologically driven change. It also provides the backbone for the entrepreneurs in us to take risks and capitalize on the opportunities sprouted by new technologies. Simple rich people across the globe are looking at these opportunities and making bets on themselves for their way of life and those whom they love and provide for. Simplicity and clarity with money management will prepare you for the risks and changes that technologies such as AI will bring.

Simple rich people also keep their eyes open for how technologies can benefit them as consumers. Prices of many products and especially services are reduced by innovative companies that curious and open-minded consumers leverage to improve their quality of life. Simple rich people leverage technology to invest in themselves and prepare themselves for favorable financial and quality of life outcomes. A defining outcome of simplicity is an increased risk tolerance and openness to new adventures that life presents us with. Enter the lair. Embrace AI. Experiment with AI. You just gained a copilot to fly your plane.

# CHAPTER 14

# THE LONG ROAD

The road to riches can feel sluggish. As life turns and twists, new challenges befuddle the protagonist. The protagonist seeks an anchor in the storm, and the principles of money and the strength of financial empowerment are as strong an anchor as any.

The principles laid out in this book can be applied to any life. Whether it is a homeless person, a college student, or an accomplished entrepreneur, using the principles of personal finance can help you get to your State of Zen. Attaining peace does not result from race for possessions with neighbors and relatives. If there is ever any meaningful comparison, it is only with ourselves of yesterday. A person on the path to a better state should compare only with yesterday's version of the same person. To compare with another is immediately setting us up for failure, because our mindset is focusing externally outside our direct control and influence, and not inward, where we have control over variables such as where we shop, what we eat, how often we engage in vigorous physical activity, etc.

Another person also has different genes and a different family structure; these and other circumstances influence their current state, accomplishments, goals, and desires. I am not suggesting that positive habits cannot be learned from another person. The ability to learn from another and then apply it to your setting is one of the cornerstones of learning and applied intelligence. The willingness and ability to learn are reflective of a higher maturity. It is the banal comparison that is unproductive. To learn how someone avoids unnecessary snacking in the late evenings to nip this habit in the bud is good. Worrying oneself about how another looks so much better or chiseled compared to one's own shape is not.

The same philosophy applies to growth and development in managing personal finances. Meaningful personal finance goals develop from perspectives gained from introspection and reflection. This inward process connects you with the person you are, guiding you to the person you want to become. It is unnecessary and unproductive to compare with your friends, neighbors, or Instagram influences. Learn from all, but only compare to yourself from yesterday. Your personal finance situation is a product of your circumstances and behaviors until now. Your personal finance situation five years from now will be significantly shaped by the incremental habits and behaviors over the next five years, plus how fortune in life treats you. You have direct control over your habits and behaviors and can exert influence in varying capacities over the systems that influence your habits and behaviors.

The road to Z is littered with dynamics and circumstances outside our control. The burden is heavier with the baggage of expectations. Make this a journey about self-learning and learning the world around you, and the trip will be rewarding and fulfilling. There is a pot of gold in this journey, which is the journey itself. It is not what happens at the end but what will happen to you, the protagonist, on the path to liberation. Life will throw curveballs at you. Your goal shouldn't always be to avoid the curveballs but at times to ride with it.

The most beautiful roads traverse through the rainforest, those patches of land that are traveled least by most travelers. The State of Z is an inner state of curiosity, openness, hope, and courage. The road to success in personal finance is a road of truth about ourselves and the systems we live in. I encourage you to think of this journey as an experimentation and exploration of yourself and the systems you are a part of. Be curious. Be honest. Become an observer.

Create a discipline of budgeting, and manage your finances with care. During my journey, there have been many times I have experimented with the systems I espouse in this book. The north star of personal finance has remained consistent, to categorize and monitor how expenses are adding value to my life and how these resources are furthering the goals I aspire to. Am I deploying my resources to shape the person I want to become? The first steps in this journey are setting goals for spending categories and tracking and monitoring expenses to strategically deploy resources toward executing plans that fulfill personal aspirations.

The time it takes you to start these efforts will whittle down as you repeat the process a few times. These efforts will result in long-term physical and mental well-being. Living within your means will provide you with a strength unbeknownst to most. The most important benefit of living a financially conscious life will not be sufficiently reflected in an increase in wealth; that will be an outcome. The feeling of richness spurred by self-reliance is the elixir. It is not only the money you will gain but the luxuriance of life you will experience, the reward of a well-lived life.

And in time, you will embody the values of simple rich people. You will look back with poise and confidence and then look forward to continuing more of the journey with an insatiable hunger for what life has to offer and a curiosity to ride with life's plans.

Continue the conversation at www.simplerichpeople.com
TikTok - simplerichpeople

# BIBLIOGRAPHY

1 American Psychological Association. "2014 Stress in America Survey."

2 https://www.wsj.com/articles/it-now-costs-300-000-to-raise-a-child-11660864334

3 https://www.genworth.com/aging-and-you/finances/cost-of-care.html

4 Wood, W., Quinn, J. M., & Kashy, D. A. (2002). Habits in everyday life: Thought, emotion, and action. Journal of Personality and Social Psychology, 83(6), 1281–1297.

5 https://www.investopedia.com/articles/taxes/08/tax-loss-harvesting.asp

6 https://www.statista.com/chart/16434/james-bond-product-placements/#:~:text=In%20the%201960s%2C%20Bond%20films,anything%20from%20alcohol%20to%20cars

7 https://www.forbes.com/sites/priceonomics/2018/07/10/heres-how-much-money-do-you-save-by-cooking-at-home/?sh=8f7684835e54

[8] https://njaes.rutgers.edu/sshw/message/message.php?p=Finance&m=343

[9] https://www.businessinsider.com/studies-help-explain-why-credit-cards-make-us-spend-more-2014-7

[10] https://www.apa.org/news/press/releases/stress/2022/concerned-future-inflation

[11] https://www.ncbi.nlm.nih.gov/pmc/articles/PMC8425299/

[12] https://www.ramseysolutions.com/relationships/money-marriage-communication-research

[13] https://www.creditkarma.com/credit-cards/i/credit-card-minimum-payment

[14] https://www.mckinsey.com/featured-insights/diversity-and-inclusion/women-in-the-workplace

Printed in the USA
CPSIA information can be obtained
at www.ICGtesting.com
LVHW051119190424
777773LV00002B/17